INFORMATION AND TECHONOLOGIES IN AFRICA

Volume 2

The experience with community telecentres

Edited by
Florence Ebam Etta and Sheila Parvyn-Wamahiu

International Development Research Centre
Ottawa • Dakar • Cairo • Montevideo • Nairobi • New Delhi • Singapore

Council for the Development of Social Science Research in Africa

© International Development Research Centre 2003

Jointly published by the International Development Research Centre (IDRC)
PO Box 8500, Ottawa, ON, Canada K1G 3H9
http://www.idrc.ca

and the Council for the Development of Social Science Research in Africa
(CODESRIA)
PO Box 3304, Dakar, Senegal
http://www.codesria.org
ISBN 2-86978-115-6

National Library of Canada cataloguing in publication data
Main entry under title:
Information and communication technologies for development in Africa.
Volume 2: The experience with community telecentres

Co-published by CODESRIA.
ISBN 1-55250-006-3

1. Information technology – Africa.
2. Communication in community development – Africa.
3. Community development – Africa.
I. Etta, Florence Ebam.
II. Parvyn-Wamahiu, Sheila.
III. International Development Research Centre (Canada)
IV. Codesria.

HC805.I55I53 2003   338.9'26'096   C2003-980280-9

All rights reserved. No part of this publication may be reproduced, stored in a retrieval system, or transmitted, in any form or by any means, electronic, mechanical, photocopying, or otherwise, without the prior permission of the International Development Research Centre. Mention of a proprietary name does not constitute endorsement of the product and is given only for information.

Contents

List of figures vi
List of tables vii
List of acronyms and abbreviations ix
Foreword xii
Preface xiv
Acknowledgements xvi
Executive summary xvii

Chapter 1

Introduction: Joining the information society

Purpose 5
Background 7
Research issues 10
Methodology 11
Key concepts 12
Structure 14

Chapter 2

ICTs in Africa: The landscape for growing telecentres

Introduction 17
ICTs in Africa: Context and background 20
ICT equipment and other contextual factors 27
Toward universal service: Telecentres and public access ... 29
Definition and development of telecentres 30
Glimpses from the literature 32
Conclusion 34

Chapter 3

Timbuktu telecentre, Mali

Telecommunications context	37
Timbuktu	38
Findings	40
Sustainability	52
Summary and conclusion	58

Chapter 4

Telecentres in Mozambique

Telecommunications context	59
Telecentre context	60
Telecentre locations	61
Profile of users	61
Equipment and services offered	63
Management, ownership, and sustainability	69
Conclusion and recommendations	69

Chapter 5

Telecentres in Uganda

Telecommunications context	72
Telecentre context	75
Findings	78
Access	82
Service delivery	88
Impediments to use	91
Relevance	94
Ownership, management, and sustainability	103
Conclusion	113

Chapter 6

Telecentres in South Africa

Telecommunication context	115
Study sites	114
Findings	119
Relevance	123
Ownership, management, and sustainability	123
Conclusion	126

Chapter 7

Telecentres in Senegal

Telecommunications context	127
Context of telecentres	130
Findings	131
Relevance	139
Management, ownership, and sustainability	140
Summary and conclusion	148

Chapter 8

Conclusion

The political, socio-economic, and technological contexts	151
Access: Emerging pictures	154
Impediments to use	158
Relevance of telecentres	161
Ownership, management, and sustainability	162
Conclusion: Whither community telecentres?	166

Appendices	171
Bibliography	181

Figures

Figure 1. Timbuktu telecentre users for selected months 43
Figure 2. Service used by sex in Manhiça and Namaacha 64
Figure 3. Location of community telecentres, Uganda 77
Figure 4. Percentage use of the services offered at the three
  telecentres 84
Figure 5. Men and women registered users of community telecentres.. 87
Figure 6. Observed usage of telecentres 88
Figure 7. Telecentre income in FCFA 147
Figure 8. Telecentre expenditure in FCFA 147

Tables

Table 1. Acacia-supported telecentres in sub-Saharan Africa 5
Table 2. Internet users as percentage of total population 24
Table 3. Inventory of telecentre equipment 41
Table 4. Inventory of software 42
Table 5. Number of users in Timbuktu telecentre 44
Table 6. Distance travelled, method of transport, and time taken to reach various sources of information in Timbuktu 46
Table 7. Types of information, service used, and cost of using Telecentre 48
Table 8. Common technical problems encountered at the telecentre ... 49
Table 9. Community involvement in telecentre management 54
Table 10. Telecentre revenue (1999 to 2001) 56
Table 11. Sex of telecentre users in Manhiça and Namaacha 62
Table 12. Age of telecentre users in Manhiça and Namaacha 63
Table 13. Frequency of use of telecentre services by men and women...65
Table 14. Service used by sex in Manhiça and Namaacha 67
Table 15. Telecommunications indicators 74
Table 16. Facilities at community telecentres and private cybercafés 78
Table 17. Equipment available and in actual use in the telecentres and cybercafés 79
Table 18. Services offered at each of the telecentres and cybercafes ... 81
Table 19. Percentage of services used 85
Table 20. Frequency of technical problems and how they were handed 89
Table 21. Purpose of last visit 95
Table 22. Where there is no telecentre 98
Table 23. Staffing patterns at telecentres and cybercafes 105

vii

Table 24. Nature of community involvement in management of community telecentres 107
Table 25. Staff responsibility for expenditures 110
Table 26. Estimated monthly income and expenditures (in UGS) by service type 112
Table 27. Length of telecentre use 133
Table 28. Sex of users 135
Table 29. Age of users 135
Table 30. Contacts maintained through the telecentres with others in Dakar, Senegal, Africa, the rest of the world 137
Table 31. Monthly incomes and expenditures at three types of telecentres in Senegal 144

Acronyms and abbreviations

AISI	African Information Society Initiative
ANC	African National Congress
ART	Agence de Régulation des Télécommunications
ASC	Associations Sportives et Culturelles
BRACO	IDRC Regional Office for West Africa
C-Band	Broadcast Spectrum
CAL	Local Advisory Committees (Mozambique Telecentres)
CBO	Community Based Organization
CCTAS	Community Centre for Health-Related Technology
CDG	Carl Duisberg Gesellschaft
CD-ROM	Compact Disk Read Only Memory
CIUEM	Eduardo Mondlane University Informatics Centre
CODEL	Local Development Committee (Senegal)
CODESRIA	Council for the Development of Social Science Research in Africa
CRC	Community Resource Centre
CTA	European Commission for Technical Cooperation in Agriculture for African, Caribbean and Pacific countries
DSTV	Digital Satellite Television
ECOPOP	Economie populaire urbaine (Program of ENDA)
EDM	Mozambique Electricity Company
EIG	Economic Interest Group
ELSA	Evaluation and Learning System for Acacia
ENDA	Environmental Development Action in the Third World (NGO)
FAO	UN Food and Agriculture Organization
FGD	Focus Group Discussion
FCFA	Franc, currency issued by Central Bank of West African States
GDP	Gross Domestic Product

GNP	Gross National Product
GPF	Promotion of Women's Interests Group
GSM	Global System for Mobile Communications
IBA	Independent Broadcasting Authority
ICASA	Independent Communications Authority of South Africa
ICT	Information and communication technology
IDRC	International Development Research Centre
IICD	International Institute for Communication and Development
ISDN	Integrated Switched Digital Network
ISP	Internet Service Provider
IT	Information Technology
ITU	International Telecommunication Union
IP	Internet Protocol
ITU	International Telecommunications Union
LAN	Local Area Network
MCT	Multipurpose Community Telecentre
MTN	Mobile Telephone Networks (South African Company)
NEPAD	New Partnership for African Development
NGO	Non-governmental Organization
NICI	National Information and Communication Infrastructure
PC	Personal Computer
PCM	Pulse Coded Modulation
POP	Internet Point of Presence
PSTN	Public Switched Telephone Networks
PTO	Post and Telecommunications Offices
RCDF	Rural Communications Development Fund
SANCO	South African National Civic Organization
SATRA	South Africa Telecom Regulatory Authority
SMS	Short Messaging Service
SONATEL	Société Nationale de Télécommunication (National Telecommunications Company, Senegal)
SOTELMA	Société de Télécommunication de Mali (Telecommunications Company, Mali)
TC	Telecentre
TDM	Mozambique Telecommunications Company
TPS	Trade Point Senegal
UCC	Uganda Communications Commission

UNCST	Uganda National Council of Science and Technology
UNDP	UN Development Programme
UNESCO	United Nations Educational, Scientific, and Cultural Organization
UNIN	University of the North (South Africa)
UPL	Uganda Posts Limited
UPS	Uninterruptible Power Supply
UPTC	Uganda Posts and Telecommunications Corporation
USA	Universal Service Agency (South Africa)
USAID	US Agency for International Development
USD	United States Dollar
UTL	Uganda Telecom
VCR	Video Cassette Recorder
VSAT	Very Small Aperture Terminal (satellite communications terminal)
WAN	Wide Area Network
WAP	Wireless Application Protocol
WASC	West African Submarine Cable
WWW	World Wide Web
ZAR	South African Rand

Foreword

By the 1990s, the world was said to be firmly in the information age, and talk of an information revolution was rife. The world also awakened to the real possibility of a global information divide whose contours would mirror those of existing economic prosperity. World attention was drawn to the potential of information and communications technologies (ICTs) to make real changes in ensuring prosperity. Following the heightened crisis in African development in the late 1980s, and the painfully unsuccessful efforts to remedy economic performance through structural adjustment programmes, this potential was welcome news. This new remedy for the eradication of poverty ignited widespread interest among visionaries and set the pace and tone for the new directions and for a number of notable events.

The 1996 Midrand, South Africa, conference on the Information Society for African Development was one such event. As a direct consequence of this conference, the Acacia Initiative was launched by IDRC. In form and spirit, the Acacia Initiative was bold and unique. When it was launched in 1997, Acacia was the single largest program of the Centre. Fittingly, an African, Gaston Zongo, with deep understanding for the politics, operations and ICT infrastructure of much of the continent, was the first chief executive of Acacia.

Five years later, IDRC has invested more than 20 million Canadian dollars in almost three hundred projects. Owing to their visibility and potential for mass impact, the telecentre projects have received attention and popular acclaim. These projects also provided IDRC with the opportunity to enter into practical project-level partnerships with the International Telecommunications Union, UNESCO, and others at a time when partnering among donors was seen as a growing necessity. The publishing partnership between the Council for the Development of Social Science Research in Africa (CODESRIA) and IDRC for this book, as well as the other volumes in this series, is testimony to the continuing need for collaboration among development partners.

Since the mid-1990s, proclamations regarding the transformative power and potential of ICTs have been persistently made by a growing band of powerful and influential individuals and organizations. But at a meeting in London, England, late in 2001, experts discussing technology and poverty lamented that amazingly little concrete evidence existed to support these claims. At that meeting, and doubtless many others where the issue has been discussed, one of the recommendations was to gather the information needed to show whether these technologies work, and how they work for the poor. This book tries to do just that. It also illustrates that much still remains to be learnt and understood about the relationship between public access, of which telecentres are but one example, and development, as we know it.

It is our hope that the glimpses provided in this book will incite further study and stimulate investments in telecentres since they hold much promise for a large number of people in the developing world.

Adebayo Olukoshi
Executive Secretary
CODESRIA

Maureen O'Neil
President
IDRC

Preface

Africa is now creating its own Information Society. How the opportunities and challenges of this transformation play out within African communities will be fascinating to learn from and to observe. This volume is intended to contribute to this process.

The African inspiration and imagination can find new expression with the digital tools that so many in the world now take for granted. The computer, the printer, the digital camera, email and the Internet have become essential tools for living and working for many. But this was not always the case. What is now the Internet first began in 1970 and the first personal computer entered the market in 1981. Despite this, email, the Internet and all that followed from it did not really enter the mainstream of industrial life until the mid-1990s.

Many African communities are now entering the first wave of experiential learning and adoption of digital technologies in education, health, business and government. As was the case when the first telecentre in the North was established in Velmdalen, Sweden in 1985, digital pioneers are stepping forward to ensure that the enabling effects, which these technologies can have, become widely available.

The case studies included in this volume speak to the efforts of African digital pioneers who were driven to use telecentres as a mechanism to launch the African Information Revolution in their own countries and communities. Their dedication and perseverance is an inspiration. We trust that these case studies honour and respect their time, courage and sacrifice in what they have tried to accomplish.

These case studies are also but a small expression of the many people who contributed to the first generation of IDRC's Acacia program. They too were digital pioneers and, as is so often the case with inspired heresy, some experienced the singe of orthodox convention.

As more international agencies come to integrate digital technologies as a component of their programming, the experiences reflected in these case studies are especially pertinent and germane. We appreciate the dedication of the researchers who prepared these. We also look forward to the other expressions of what has been learned from the Acacia experience as they become available.

    Richard Fuchs
    Director
    Information and Communication Technologies for Development
    International Development Research Centre

Acknowledgements

We express sincere appreciation to very many people, too many to name individually, who contributed to making this book possible including all the partners, principal researchers, data collectors, interviewees, and workshop participants in all five countries. The research, mandated by the senior management committee of the International Development Research Centre, conceptualized by the entire Acacia team was conducted and reported by a dedicated group of principal researchers in each of the five countries in the study sample: Khamathe Sene, Babacar Bah and Bureau d'Etudes de conseils et d'intervention au Sahel (BECIS) in Mali; Carlos Cumbana and Esselina Macome in Mozambique; Mor Dieng, Khamathe Sene, and Pape Touty Sow in Senegal; Peter Benjamin, M. E. Maepa, A. Molefe, and R. Ramagogodi in South Africa; and Samuel Kayabwe, Richard Kibombo, Esther Nakazze, and Stella Neema in Uganda. All those who contributed to this book and therefore deserve to be acknowledged are listed in Appendix I.

We also wish to place on record our gratitude to Caroline Pestieau, former Vice-President, IDRC, Connie Freeman, Regional Director of the Eastern and Southern Africa Regional Office of IDRC, who provided much needed support and motivation for a long and difficult task.

We acknowledge with appreciation the insights, observations, contributions and support of the Interim Team leader Acacia, Laurent Elder, Ramata Molo Thioune, Terry Smutylo, Director IDRC Evaluation Unit and Bill Carman of IDRC. The Acacia team bears no responsibility for any shortcomings, errors or misinterpretations. This responsibility rests with the principal researchers for the respective national studies and the editors of this volume.

Florence E. Etta
Sheila Parvyn-Wamahiu

Executive summary

It is incontestable that the information and knowledge age is here, and has been with humankind since the last decades of the second millennium. This age is characterised by economic globalization and the new Information and Communication Technologies (ICTs). ICTs are regarded as the engines of the new economy driving a new information and economic world order in which information-rich countries have the heaviest and most sophisticated ICT use. Most of the continent of Africa is not faring too well on either indicator – i.e., availability or use. Momentum has been gathering in the last half-decade on a global scale to support the development, diffusion, use and appropriation of ICTs in knowledge-poor countries and regions in Africa and Asia in particular. One of the ways this is being done is through the establishment of community telecentres also known as public access points.

The telecentre movement on the continent is young. The earliest community telecentres are reputed to have opened their doors in 1998. The nature and functions of African telecentres vary slightly from country to country, so too do the names and labels by which they are known. The primary goal of a telecentre, is the public provision of tools and skills to enhance communication and the sharing of information. A number of administrative and operational arrangements are possible, and although community telecentres can be organizationally differentiated from franchises and cybercafés they are all functionally of the same genre. Whatever the management model, there is general consensus that the telecentre concept is a valid development tool.

All the significant indicators of development in a knowledge-based digital world, i.e., levels of general literacy, scientific and technical literacy, number of computers, newspapers, radios, television sets, telephones etc. show that Africa is not doing well at this moment in history. The patterns of availability of the instruments and tools for knowledge creation, and information sharing are also unfortunately not evenly distributed among the populations. Rural areas and their inhabitants are usually disadvantaged in their access to information and communication technologies. Following the rise in the rhetoric on human rights, of equality and equity accompanied by the growing activism within civil society in defence of these rights, governments (national and international) have had to respond to the disparity in access between the rich and the poor, educated and illiterate, urban and rural dwellers, to information and communication tools, which are so important for contemporary existence.

The telecentre is one answer to the prevailing condition of uneven and unequal access to information and communication technologies in rural and or remote areas. The telecentre has economic and social justification. Owing to the levels of poverty of both governments and individuals, prospects for private individual purchase of information and communication tools are particularly bleak. It therefore makes economic sense to provide equipment on a multi-user, multi-service basis as a means of spreading costs while simultaneously expanding access and benefits. Governments customarily have the duty to provide for and support the development of all citizens, and although rural areas have long suffered neglect with respect to telecommunications networks, in a global climate of growing militancy for equality, this disadvantage and bias are creating growing irritation in need of attention.

Beginning in the mid-1990s, the International and Development Research Centre among like-minded organizations such as the International Telecommunications Union and UNESCO to mention a few, invested time, effort and money to investigate this phenomenon of potential importance. In the earlier part of this engagement, because of the paucity of projects, much of the effort was spent in intervention-type projects in a handful of African countries, establishing telecentre-type facilities and structures in schools, in rural settings, hospitals etc. This was geared towards spreading knowledge and familiarity of the new information and communication tools. Although by historical accounts, the telecentre is a relatively new institution in Africa, and indeed the world and still surrounded by many unknowns, it is believed that as a delivery model for ICTs, telecentres have the potential to transform the lives and livelihoods of many in the developing world and especially those in remote rural locations in developing countries.

Background

The diffusion of new ICTs on the African continent is not extensive because of the recency of their introduction. The continent's entry and participation in the information society and revolution can be said to have commenced in the mid-1990s with the call for an African Information Society. In 1996, African ministers and governments endorsed the African Information Society Initiative (AISI) as the framework within which to build Africa's information and communications infrastructure. Acacia, initiated in 1997, was Canada's response to and support for that call.

The Acacia Initiative was designed as an integrated programme of research and development that used demonstration projects to address issues of information and communications technology, infrastructure, policy, and applications.

The original objectives of Acacia included:

- A demonstration of how information and communication technologies can enable communities to solve development problems in ways that build upon local goals, cultures, strengths, and processes; and
- The construction of a validated body of knowledge and a networked dissemination process around effective approaches, policies, technologies, and methodologies.

Acacia's original vision was to target disadvantaged and mainly rural communities, which were isolated from information and communication networks, and the marginalized groups within these communities, in particular, youth and women. A key element of this vision was to use information and communication technologies in the search for solutions to local development problems. Acacia's initial implementation strategy of working in a select group of countries was informed by the limited funding available to guarantee focused learning in a short time period. Between 1997 and 2000, Acacia concentrated its work in four sub-Saharan African countries; namely, Mozambique, Senegal, South Africa, and Uganda although a few projects were implemented in others, e.g., Mali, Benin, and Tanzania. Acacia has since been involved with a total of 35 telecentres in seven countries in sub-Saharan Africa, five of which have been jointly funded with other international partners such as UNESCO and ITU among others.

This volume "The Experience with Community Telecentres" presents the results of a series of studies that examined the setting, operations and effects of community telecentres. The studies reported in this book were planned and conducted as evaluative research to make a contribution towards illuminating the relationship of ICTs and development in the continent. The rationale for the studies was the consolidation of learning from telecentre and telecentre-type projects in Africa, in order to share this learning widely and contribute to an understanding of the issues and prospects for telecentre development on the continent. At the time of the launch of the Acacia initiative in 1997, the general opinion concerning investments in ICTs in Africa was very unsupportive and hostile and very different from the contemporary picture of global endorsement and acceptance that ICTs are critical for fast and future development.

Method

The studies were conducted in Mali, Mozambique, Senegal, South Africa and Uganda using a similar methodology. In keeping with the spirit of learning and stakeholder participation as key elements, the studies commenced with an interactive and participatory research-design workshop held in August 2000. This was meant to meet two goals. Firstly, it ensured that the principal stakeholders shared their understanding and expectations of the evaluation research process, and secondly, it helped guarantee buy-in for the research results. Ownership and buy-in were considered important because the results were to be ploughed back into the management and practices of the telecentre projects.

National research teams in each of the countries adapted centrally developed instruments for local use. Research findings were discussed at dissemination workshops to validate the research results as well as enrich the interpretation of findings.

The studies addressed four major issues:

- Access
- Relevance
- Sustainability (ownership, management, etc)
- Environments (technological, social, economic, and political).

The following research questions formed the basis of the investigations:

- What is the nature of access to ICTs within the telecentres?
- How relevant, useful and appropriate are the services, content and applications offered or available at the telecentres to community members and how well do the services, content and applications meet community needs?
- What are the ownership and management models and how have these contributed to the sustainability of community telecentres? What other factors affect sustainability?
- What is the nature of the social, economic, political, and technological context within which the telecentres operate?

The studies used a robust methodology that included both qualitative and quantitative methods to collect data from actual and potential telecentre users in the communities. These methods included focus group discussions, naturalistic or realistic observations, in-depth case histories and key-informant interviews, user interviews, document analysis, and photo documentation.

The primary sample consisted of the telecentres themselves. A total of thirty-six telecentres and cybercafés were sampled; five in Uganda, three in Mali, two in Mozambique, six in South Africa, and twenty in Senegal. The survey samples included users and potential users around the telecentres. The criteria used for selecting the telecentres included: their location (rural or urban), ownership type (private, franchise or donor-funded), services offered, and telecentre maturity. Telecentres that had been operating for less than 12 months were not investigated. The total number of individuals who provided information in all the countries was 3,586. The studies were conducted between mid 2000 and late 2001.

Key findings

Access

Use

Undoubtedly, the telecentres have brought a large number of people in disadvantaged and under-served – often rural communities – into direct contact with modern ICTs. This familiarization would not have been possible had the telecentre projects not been embarked upon in the first place. However only a still small percentage of the total population was using the telecentre facilities. The numbers of daily visitors ranged from about 8 to 20 for each TC and some visitors made more than one trip to the facilities.

It was found that age, sex, education and literacy levels, and socioeconomic status influenced telecentre use. A striking observation was the absence of old and disabled people at the telecentres.

Fewer women than men use telecentre services in practically all of the countries and facilities. This finding confirms the poor standing of African women in science and technology, a consistent and now familiar reality. In Mali, 77% of the users were men, and at Manhiça in Mozambique, 63% of the users were men. The trend in Senegal and Uganda was similar. In Senegal 70% of users were men.

Education appeared to be a key determinant of telecentre use. A popular belief expressed by respondents was that telecentre services were for the elite or educated. In Mozambique, at least 50% of the users had secondary level education, and 63% of all users were students. In Uganda, university undergraduates, teachers and students made up the largest percentage of users. In Mali, speakers of Arabic were disadvantaged.

Telecentre benefits spread to a wider section of the population than simply to direct users, as it was common practice to share information with others.

Location greatly affected accessibility and the use of facilities in some telecentres. Additional costs for transportation to get to the telecentre, and perceived threats and security of users associated with the location, reduced use.

Services

The telecentres in all five countries offered similar services: photocopying, telephony, and training in computer hardware, software, Internet access, and word processing. Facsimile transmission; document design, processing, and printing; and email services were also available. The huge popularity of the telephone is undisputed. The range of services offered in the multipurpose community telecentres was wider than in the private telecentres or cybercafés. However, the level of use made of this wider array of services was lower. Low or non-use of some services was reported, for example, Internet and email in the more rural TCs in Uganda, Mozambique, and Mali.

Most of the telecentres experienced management problems, ranging from poor attitudes, to weak management, and technical skills.

Impediments to use

Cost of services. Users expressed concern about fees charged for services. The high cost of services in relation to user incomes and earnings was identified as a serious barrier for women, the unemployed, students and poor community members.

Cost of equipment, maintenance and supplies. The high cost of equipment, supplies and maintenance, e.g., cost of computers, software licenses and cartridges for inkjet printers, electricity, telephones (and the charges) and the common practice of getting technicians from far away places for either routine maintenance or repairs was a constant heavy burden to carry which affected use. These costs are usually reflected in service charges.

Inadequate physical facilities. Usually the available space was either too small or poorly managed with little privacy for users of the telephones or other equipment. Most TCs were operating from premises that had been converted from other uses.

Poor management. Most of the telecentres experienced some management problems, ranging from poor attitudes, to weak management, technical and even social skills. The quality and number of staff was inadequate and marked by the use of poorly trained staff and volunteers with weak remuneration.

Hours of operation. The telecentres keep formal government working hours, which limit the time during which the facilities are open to the public. Facilities were usually not open late, at night, on Sundays, or during public holidays.

Inappropriate location. Location greatly affected accessibility and the use of facilities in some of the telecentres. Additional costs, such as for transportation to get to the telecentre, and perceived threats to the users (i.e. safety/security), or discomfort associated with the location, reduced use.

Poor publicity. Not enough seems to have been done to create awareness about either the locations of the telecentres or the services offered by them.

Literacy and language. The telecentres are perceived as places providing services for the educated on account of the language of the content, most of which is in English.

Relevance

The main reason for using the telecentres was to obtain or send information and for the most part the purpose of this information was social: for contacting friends and family, for preparing documents for social events (e.g., weddings and funerals), and for personal entertainment, such as watching television and videos, listening to radio, or reading newspapers. Professional and economic motives, such as seeking economic and agricultural information, came a distant second on the list of reasons for telecentre use. Telecentres facilitated business or commercial transactions for a small percentage of users in Uganda (10–20%). In some instances TCs were used as meeting places, as places of shelter/safety as well as for training groups of women etc.

Users expressed satisfaction with the services offered pointing out that the telecentres had opened them and their communities to wider audiences, facilitated external communication, and promoted knowledge of computer technology among local community members.

Ownership, management, and sustainability

Three ownership models were evident: private (individual) ownership, private NGO or CBO ownership and trusteeship. No public facility was represented in the sample. The franchise model seen in South Africa with the Universal Service Agency (USA) is regarded as a variant of private ownership. Most of the community TCs investigated were in the category of trusteeship. This is an arrangement where the project is being held in trust by the executing agency for a specified period of time during the lifetime of the project until the final owner – i.e., the community – is ready to take it over at which point it might become a public facility if taken over by a government department or institution. There were indications of movement in this direction with some of the older projects in Uganda.

Management was usually the responsibility of project staff, local management committees and the project implementation agency. The extent of involvement of the local committees usually represented on the management committees was not always clear and their level of responsibility often did not extend beyond supporting fund-raising and mobilization for the TCs. Most of the control was vested in the project-executing agencies, whether these were universities, ministries or governmental agencies.

Sustainability

Whereas conceptual validity has given meaning and a measure of institutional relevance and validity to the telecentre idea, financial sustainability for community telecentres remains elusive. Only two examples of sustainable community TCs were found in Phalala (South Africa) and Guédiawaye (Senegal).

The financial sustainability of TCs was under constant threat not only from weak management but also from recurrent technical and infrastructure problems in all countries. These problems included: power failures or interruptions; poor connectivity; computer failures; printer breakdowns; non-functioning software; obsolete or unusable equipment; complex management arrangements, security failure and policy failures, e.g., import duties or taxes on equipment. Some telecentres in Uganda and Senegal, for example, had to go through considerable bureaucratic hurdles simply to have imported equipment released to projects or simply repaired.

Technological environment

The greatest threat to TC sustainability was technical and technological. In addition to the generally poor telecommunications infrastructure, the overall state of infrastructure continues to be a source of great concern, particularly with regard to unreliable or non-existent electricity supply.

Although privatisation has proceeded apace, state-owned or state-controlled telecommunications service providers still enjoy relative monopolies and exclusivity privileges. Little real competition exists for the provision of fixed-line services. As a direct consequence, tariffs remain high and infrastructure development in rural areas stultified. Competition exits in cellular and wireless telephony and this creates other types of problems for telecentres, e.g., urban bias, higher costs etc.

Existing social and political institutions and policies are young and therefore weak to support the development, spread and widespread adoption of ICTs. The fragile economic situation of much of the continent is well documented.

Recommendations

General

On account of the huge unmet demand (need) for information and communication, the nature and extent of poverty, the slow and uneven pace of development of delivery tools and mechanisms, especially to rural areas where the majority of Africans still reside, the telecentre has a certain and definite role and place in contemporary development.

The telecentre is to information what the school is to education and the hospital or clinic to health and well-being.

- Support should therefore be given to start, maintain and run telecentres because they perform a primary development function for information and education, which is considered a basic and important human right.
- International development agencies and multilateral, bilateral and national agencies should support the development and growth of telecentres. This means, for example, extending the project lifespan; since shorter project cycles are insufficient to adequately support the optimal development of telecentres.

Optimising the development of telecentres will ensure that the telecentre movement can grow, spread and have the expected or desired effects. For this to happen, however, the following issues, for which support is critical, must be seriously addressed: connectivity, content, capacity, costs and conceptual framework. A conceptual framework to underpin the expansion and roll-out of services is often undervalued and therefore underdeveloped or ignored, yet it is of supreme importance and ought to be the point of entry. The spread of ICTs should be based on a theory of social change, which treats exogenous and endogenous information as having equal potential value for instigating transformation and the new technologies should be used for spreading the most useful ones widely. Social change that threatens the very existence of any society or community is unwelcome. Therefore, the underlying assumption in a useful theory of social change as a framework ought to be one based on the value of information to the extent that it advances the cause of society. To build and use a framework for ICT dispersal that does not take cognizance of the geography, ethno-linguistic diversity, the economic strength and the predominant occupational pattern of the majority of inhabitants of the continent is akin to navigating with a flawed compass or worse with none. A useful strategy would be a framework that proceeds from the identified information and development needs of common folk as the base point from which to chart a path of transformation in whose service ICTs are applied. This will ensure that the starting point of deployment is grounded human need not merely technological or commercial adventurism.

- Governments and their agents must therefore invest in the articulation and development of a clear theory of inclusiveness and effectiveness to guide the development and deployment of ICTs on a large scale.
- Project designers should also have a similarly clear framework for the empowerment of users as well as non-users.

Connectivity is crucial for without it the benefits of the new information and network age cannot be harnessed. But connectivity is often beyond the direct control of telecentre operators, managers or project implementers. Connectivity relies on the telecommunications infrastructure, which is provided or controlled by nation states, their agencies, or licensed private operators.

- Telecommunications infrastructure should be seen and treated by governments as a growth area in which public and private investments ought to be encouraged.
- National governments should create enabling environments through policies and policy instruments for the growth of telecentres. Laws should be supportive not prohibitive of developments in appropriate and practical technologies. For instance, import duties and taxes on information and communication equipment, e.g., computers as well as licenses to operate equipment (VSAT), the spectrum and premises devoted to the development and delivery of information should be reasonable, realistic, easy to get and difficult to revoke.

Content and applications can be viewed as the blood that runs through the veins of connectivity or the electronic impulses travelling through a computer network. Local content is particularly valued and a monumental effort aimed at collecting, creating, collating, transforming, and uploading relevant content and applications should be supported and embarked upon

xxvii

without delay. The greatest difficulty with the creation or transformation of locally relevant and available content is human capacity. This expertise and skill base need to be created, expanded and deepened across all social and occupational strata as a matter of urgency to improve the use, service delivery and applications available at telecentres.

- Governments and development agencies should design projects to train a growing number of people and equip them with the skills required for content development and the transformation of content into multi-media formats.
- Investments should also be encouraged into experiments in applications and piloted in TCs in the areas of health, education, governance etc.

All the investments in connectivity, content, and capacity development would ultimately be meaningless if the cost of services is such that they remain unpopular, unreachable, or unusable by the majority of rural Africans. For this reason the costs associated with establishing and running telecentres ought to be reduced in order for the services to be provided at affordable rates to users.

- Government policies that influence costs and service pricing need to be implemented, e.g., import duties, taxes, broadcast operating licenses of for instance VSAT, software and hardware prices and services that cost less to deliver, e.g., Voice-over Internet protocol (VOIP) should be researched.
- Private sector IT and communications companies should consider forming creative partnerships with each other and with national governments on one hand and international development agencies and civil society organizations on the other to create cheaper products which would respond to the needs, assets and conditions of the communities served by and through telecentres. For example, a number of different service providers for say telephony, training, email, photocopying etc could band together to set up and run TCs.

Specific

Expanding access, reaching the under-served. Project developers and project managers need to design telecentres projects with current non-users in mind. This requires taking practical and strategic needs as well as realities into consideration. For example, women, older and or handicapped persons may have inhibitions about using telecentres on account of their locations, schedules services, content or physical layout, which are insensitive or perceived inappropriate.

Assuring quality, enhancing relevance, expanding choices. Telecentre services desperately need improvement; the fact that sometimes users have no viable alternative not withstanding. Areas of action include the following:

- Location. Careful choice of location taking into consideration a large number of factors that affect the use, accessibility, safety etc., of public spaces.
- Poor publicity. Awareness and sensitisation should be increased through the use of handbills, radio broadcasts of services and interactive services/product design and delivery.
- Poor management. Financial and management training should be given to staff and committee members on a regular basis as a feature of projects.

Simpler management models and, if not, clearly articulated and supportive roles for each management group or of actors should be instituted. The nature of significant relationships and responsibilities in a trustee model are still unclear and in dire need of refinement and understanding through further research.

The range of management and ownership models should be expanded. Experiments in public, private and multiple ownership arrangements could be attempted for rural and remote populations as one way of improving financial sustainability.

Better service hours and arrangements should be developed, e.g., 24-hour pre-paid services could be arranged and public sensitive working hours should be adopted. Sensitivity to public needs is a necessity for improved use e.g., time and space could be allocated for different user groups say women and younger users.

- Physical facilities. Attention should be paid to public needs e.g., booths for privacy in addition to sensitivity to human functions and functioning, e.g., availability of toilets, fans etc.
- Equipment purchase and maintenance. The cost of purchasing and maintaining equipment should be reduced through a number of schemes, e.g., tax exemption or breaks, reclassification of communications equipment, technical training for telecentre staff, volunteers and the institutionalisation or development of village technical corps in a scheme for/of technicians on foot/bicycles. The cost of equipment maintenance and management should be a subject of serious study and innovation.
- Cost of Services. Efforts should be made to develop subsidised services, group rates, e.g., for women, students, or members. Time banding where cheaper rates can be given for off-peak periods and differential pricing, e.g., for council/government offices who take services on credit or long to pay. It should also be possible to arrange for cheaper collective rates for electricity, telephone, etc., so that TC services can be correspondingly subsidised. Open source options and arrangements should be explored, researched and utilised. The current discussions and explorations in open source and free software are a welcome development even though the future impacts are unclear.
- Cost of equipment. Cheaper hardware and software should be developed, e.g., thin client solutions and TCs should be used to pilot them.
- Literacy and language. Both local and official languages should be used for operations at TCs and content in local language sourced, or translations into local languages be encouraged and supported.

Chapter 1

Introduction: Joining the information society

It is generally acknowledged that the information and knowledge age is here, and has in-fact been with humankind since the last decades of the second millennium. This age has been characterized largely by the dominance of two movements both related and in the service of an age-old human preoccupation: capitalist accumulation. Economic globalization and the new Information Communication Technologies (ICTs) are seen as the engines of contemporary global economy driving a new information world order in which most of the continent of Africa is not faring too well. Market logic largely drives the currents in these two movements and it is a real concern that the new information and knowledge society, rather than close the development and poverty gap, might in fact aggravate it; thereby, reducing the dividends of global capitalism. The notion that ICTs are pre-eminent for faster development especially in the underdeveloped South is pervasive and momentum is gathering on a global scale to support the development, diffusion, use and appropriation of ICTs in knowledge-poor countries and regions in Africa and Asia in particular.

There is little doubt that historians of civilizations will acknowledge the information revolution of the late twentieth century as having introduced significant changes in the nature of human interactions and relations between peoples and nations. Globalization and its driver the new ICTs have taken the world by storm and their message of change or be damned (read dead) is being trumpeted loudly from a multiplicity of podiums by a growing band of important personalities and organizations. All major global organizations including the United Nations through some of its major agencies, bilaterals and even national governments, notably the group of eight most industrialised countries popularly referred to as the (G8), are extolling the virtues of new information and communication technologies. They are seen as harbingers of prosperity as they can guarantee access to global markets, enable direct foreign investment, and e-commerce. ICTs have already created a new world order of digital 'haves' and 'have nots' separated by what is popularly called and referred to as the digital divide. Much contemporary effort is being geared towards reducing this divide, improving and spreading digital dividends to the information, knowledge and by extension, material-poor of the world. A multitude of efforts and projects are currently under way to bring information and communication technologies to the developing world because of the belief in their transformative potential.

In the late 1980s and 1990s, the notion and movement for ICTs was just starting a slow trickle in sub-Saharan Africa among isolated NGOs and a few nodes in universities and specialised institutions. Many development actors, governments and a sizeable proportion of social thinkers were convinced of the utter lack of wisdom (some would even go as far as to say irresponsibility) of investing in ICTs when other more deserving and acutely pressing and perhaps life-threatening areas of action such as health, education and agriculture were still in dire need. It was generally felt that the continent was unprepared, not yet ready, for ICTs; a feeling which still persists today even among very educated, well placed and arguably well informed Africans. This in a way is at variance with expressions of faith in ICTs that they can support the necessary transformation in Africa and other developing countries. In a 1999 study provocatively titled "Can sub-Saharan Africa claim the 21st century," the World Bank President, James Wolfenson proclaims in the preface that "information and communications technology offers enormous opportunities for Africa to leap frog stages of development." World leaders regularly espouse this position and the newest proposal for Africa's development, the New Partnership for African Development (NEPAD) advanced by eminent African leaders recognises the central role of technology in the prospects for the continent.

Data to confirm these positions and affirmations is however scanty and some argue that emerging pictures suggest that far from spreading benefits, ICTs are spreading unequally and these "disparities exacerbate existing disparities based on location, gender, ethnicity, physical disability, age and especially, income level, and between 'rich' and 'poor' countries," (Bridges.org 2001).

It is this gap and absence of clarity in the data pictures that this volume hopes to fill and illuminate to some extent. On account of its deep concern for and engagement with knowledge generation and sharing, IDRC was naturally among the first development agencies to confront the thorny issue of information communication firstly among the community of researchers and later, between researchers and others in the developing world where most projects were implemented. In the 1980s, the Centre was described as "one of the few donor agencies with programs dedicated to enhancing information and informatics capabilities in developing countries ... with some 50 projects ... in Africa alone" (Akhtar 1990). This engagement with information and communication evolved in the 1990s into an interest in ICTs as computer-based/ computer-mediated technology became more widely available. The International Development Research Centre with its Acacia initiative, launched in 1997, is numbered among pioneer development agencies involved with implementing ICT projects in Africa.

Acacia, initiated nearly thirty years after the IDRC itself was created, was Canada's response to the call for an African Information Society Initiative (AISI), issued by African ministers and governments in 1996 as a framework within which to build Africa's information and communication infrastructure. Acacia is committed to empowering sub-Saharan African communities with the ability to apply information and communication technologies (ICTs) to their own social and economic development. The initial phase of the initiative was designed as an integrated programme of research and development that would use demonstration projects to address issues of technology, infrastructure, policy, and applications.

The original objectives of Acacia included:

- A demonstration of how information and communication technologies can enable communities to solve development problems in ways that build upon local goals, cultures, strengths, and processes; and
- The construction of a validated body of knowledge and a networked dissemination process around effective approaches, policies, technologies, and methodologies.

Acacia's original vision was focused on disadvantaged, mainly rural and remote communities, isolated from information and communication networks.

A key dimension of this vision was to use information and communication technologies in the search for solutions to local development problems and especially in support of women and the youth.

The specific outputs from Acacia were expected to include:

- Pilot projects that tested different approaches to providing community access to ICTs.
- Models that showed how community voices could be extended to reach and impact local planning and governance through the use of ICTs.
- On-the-ground applications that met local health, educational, natural resources management, and other development needs.
- Technology (software and hardware) that was adapted for local use in rural and disadvantaged communities.
- Innovative infrastructure that could extend networks at low cost.
- Research that showed how to make ICT policy, regulation, and practice friendlier to those currently disenfranchised.
- A system of continuous learning and evaluation that would demonstrate how communities could use research results more effectively.

Acacia's initial implementation strategy, informed by limited funding resources, revolved around working in a select group of countries to guarantee concentrated learning. Between 1997 and 2000, Acacia concentrated its work in four countries in sub-Saharan Africa: Mozambique, Senegal, South Africa, and Uganda although a few opportunistic projects were implemented in other countries, e.g., Mali, Benin, and Tanzania. Acacia supported a total of thirty-five telecentres in seven countries in sub-Saharan Africa, five of which were jointly funded with other international partners such as UNESCO and ITU (See Table 1).

Since its inception in 1997 the Acacia initiative has executed close to 300 individual projects in ICT policy, connectivity, content and applications in health, education, commerce, agriculture etc. More information about Acacia projects can be found on the website: www.idrc.ca/acacia. To date the most popular of these projects have been Schoolnets and telecentres.

Table 1. Acacia-supported telecentres in sub-Saharan Africa

Region/Country	Telecentre
East Africa	
Uganda	Nakaseke Multi-Purpose Community Telecentre (MCT)* Nabweru Buwama
Tanzania	Sengerama MCT project*
Southern Africa	
South Africa	Telecentres with Universal Service Agency (12)
Mozambique	Namaacha MCT pilot project* Namaacha telecentre Manhica telecentre
West Africa	
Senegal	Community centres with ENDA (8) Community centres with Trade Point (6)
Benin	Malanville MCT pilot project*
Mali	Timbuktu MCT pilot project*

* Jointly supported by IDRC, ITU and UNESCO. Source: IDRC, Eastern and Southern Africa Regional Office.

Purpose

In the late 1990s, the telecentre movement was just starting a slow trickle in sub-Saharan Africa after having been born a little over a decade earlier in Sweden. Few development actors were implementing ICT projects and a large number of people felt that investing in ICTs was inappropriate.

The primary aim of the studies reported in this book is therefore to inform. Most contemporary observers of the subject would admit that research on the impact of new ICTs on African development is not extensive because of their recent introduction and the rapid evolution of computer-based technologies. The book presents the results of a series of studies that examined the setting, operations and effects of community telecentres.

The studies reported in this book were planned and conducted as evaluative research to make a contribution towards illuminating the situation of ICT and development in the continent. In the conduct of the research, the advice and exhortation of Anne Whyte was heeded and the research was done "according to scientific practice so that it can withstand the scrutiny of governments and ... sceptical public and private investors" (Whyte 2000).

The design and conduct of the studies were geared towards evaluating and examining how well the African telecentre experiment was working in light of the scepticism that greeted their introduction. The studies were an attempt to establish what had been learned since the launch of the Acacia Initiative in 1997 and to identify the improvements needed to guarantee success. Whereas the rationale for the studies was the consolidation of learning from telecentre and telecentre-type projects in Africa, the rationale for this book is to share this learning widely and contribute to an understanding of the issues and prospects for telecentres on the continent.

The book describes the experiences of local and often rural communities with telecentres exploring the management structures and mechanisms that have been established to support them and provides pictures of telecentre usage. The potential and challenges of setting up and maintaining community telecentres in the context of poor information infrastructure and limited human capacity are also discussed. The contents will be useful for researchers, policy and decision makers as well as development practitioners and professionals with interests or active programs in the area of "ICT for development" and in particular those with a focus on universal access, universal service or public access centres. It will also be a very useful reference tool for academics. This book is neither a cookbook, nor a handbook. It is not a manual, which tells the reader how to run or market telecentres nor does it provide recipes for financial sustainability. For these, readers are referred to other texts e.g., Cornell University's *Handbook for Telecenter Staff* at http://ip.cals.cornell.edu/commdev/handbook or *UNESCO'S Telecentre Cookbook for Africa*.

For IDRC and Acacia, as well as for all the partners involved in the projects, the studies also provide an opportunity for extending and expanding discussions on the concepts, underlying assumptions, theory and methodologies for telecentre research. Particularly pertinent and potentially valuable would be examinations of the instruments used in the investigations reported in this book.

It is the hope of the writers and contributors, IDRC and Acacia, that this book will provide answers to some of the questions that are currently being asked or those that will in the future be asked about this area of development action and generate others.

Background

The diffusion of new ICTs on the African continent is not extensive because of the recency of their introduction. The continent's entry and participation in the information society (revolution) that can be said to have commenced in the mid-1990s is currently hampered by weak infrastructure and by material and especially policy poverty.

As a pioneer in the area of ICTs for development in Africa, Acacia was operating in largely uncharted environments. This reality informed the adoption, by the initiative, of an integrated system of research, evaluation, and learning as a central strategy and tool through which development lessons would be identified, extracted, and widely disseminated within the short lifecycles of projects. This strategy was also adopted partly on account of the nature of information and communication technologies themselves, which change rapidly and more importantly because the information was urgently needed. The luxury of long five- to ten-year experimentation periods before research or evaluation could be mounted and lessons extracted was not feasible. This embedded system for evaluation and learning was considered very innovative at the time.

The main objective of the integrated evaluation and learning strategy was to simultaneously and continuously capture learning from implemented projects and activities. These lessons were to be fed back into project processes and products. The modality for realizing this objective focussed on regular and systematic data collection along with analysis and periodic evaluations within each telecentre project, articulated at the start of the programme and was based on four pillars:

- the establishment of 'pictures' of the community that surrounded the telecentre from baseline surveys conducted at, or close to, the commencement of the telecentres;

- the development of a common set of indicators and similar evaluation frameworks for the telecentres to allow for the measurement of progress and impacts across projects;
- the institution of a system for continuous learning; and
- multi-stakeholder interaction at all levels and at regular intervals to facilitate lesson sharing, adaptation, and adoption of the telecentre model.

The evaluation and learning strategy was the method through which Acacia attempted to demonstrate the potentials as well as challenges involved with using ICTs to solve development problems in disadvantaged communities in sub-Saharan Africa. The strategy, conceptualized as a system in which learning was a central project by-product for principal implementers of the telecentres, including staff as well as users, was to bring about a significant shift in the practice of project evaluation away from a policing exercise to one in which learning, participation, and greater sharing were the principal elements. To ensure this, a sizeable proportion of each project budget was allocated to evaluation.

A number of factors operating in concert accounted for the emergence of the unique manner in which Acacia conceptualized and operationalized research, learning, and evaluation. Some of these factors included: the growing disfavour with post-hoc, externally conducted and donor-driven evaluations of development projects, the rising rhetoric for stakeholder participation, and the increasing emphasis on learning, epitomized by the preoccupation with lessons learned and the search for good practices in development discourse. The underlying philosophy of the approach was to guarantee learning by a broad spectrum of individuals within the telecentre: the staff as well as beneficiaries, the target audience, and the communities within which the facility is located. It was envisaged that the intermediaries, i.e., those institutions that act as telecentre overseers, could also learn from the projects. These institutions often represent powerful local or national interests, and because of this, learning by this group was considered an important vehicle for transforming them into knowledgeable local champions for telecentres and the telecentre movement. Donors, the international development community, and those organizations currently investing in telecentres are all looking to the outcomes of the first generation of African telecentres as a pointer to possible future fortunes or indeed misfortunes. It was therefore very important to capture learning from processes and outcomes, which were either successfully unfolding or failing.

In keeping with the spirit of the times in which learning and stakeholder participation are key elements, the studies commenced with an interactive and participatory research-design workshop. This workshop was attended by representations from a broad spectrum of stakeholders and interest groups. While it is common for experts and consultants to conduct research quite independently, using only the terms of reference drawn up by the commissioning agency as the point of contact and reference between the researcher and the institution, in the studies reported in this volume, the participation of key interest groups was maintained throughout the major stages of the research process. This accomplished two goals. Firstly, it ensured that the principal stakeholders shared their understanding and expectations of the evaluation and research process, and secondly, it helped guarantee buy-in for the research results. Ownership and buy-in were considered important because the results were to be ploughed into the management and practices of the telecentre projects. Development actors, e.g., the World Bank are currently showing a major concern for the conduct and use of evaluations by evaluated organizations, especially in Africa, and some observers have pointed out that a major determinant of the use of evaluation results is the participation of the evaluated (users) in the evaluation process (Patton 1997).

The research-design workshop, the first significant stage in the research, was held in Nairobi in August 2000 with twenty-nine participants. Participants included research associates from the Johannesburg, Dakar, and Nairobi offices of IDRC, coordinators from the multipurpose community telecentres (MCTs) in Mali and Uganda, project managers from the participating countries, representatives of donor and development institutions (UNESCO and IDRC), and representatives from the executing agencies for the projects and senior evaluation specialists, researchers, and representatives of institutional as well as individual beneficiaries of the projects. The wide array of participants was arranged to ensure that the various interest groups were directly involved in determining the evaluation issues that would form the basis for the investigations. So although in principle all the major interests were tabled at the workshop, some received scant attention during the data-gathering stages.

The principal objective of the workshop was to chart the contours of the evaluation research exercise. Consequently, it was participatory and iterative, using the 'expert' knowledge of the participants to guide the conduct and direction of the evaluation research. The major research issues and the key research questions were elaborated, as were the sample, sources, and methods of data collection. The broad design guidelines drawn up at the workshop were later used to prepare the research instruments, which the research teams used in three of the five countries. In South Africa and Mozambique, the studies were well underway when the design workshop took place, consequently, their research design differed from that used in Mali, Uganda, and Senegal. This accounts for some of the differences and similarities in the types of data and analysis presented.

National research teams in each of the countries adapted the centrally developed instruments for their local use. Training workshops were conducted for researchers and project staff in Mali, Uganda, and Senegal during which the instruments were reviewed and adapted for local use and application. Initial findings were discussed at dissemination workshops to enrich the interpretations of findings. The workshops also served to validate the research results.

Research issues

The telecentre is a relatively new institution in Africa, and indeed the world. Although still surrounded by many unknowns, it is believed that as a delivery model for ICTs, telecentres have the potential to transform the lives and livelihoods of many in the developing world and even those in remote locations in developing countries. But, the high rate of telecentre mortality witnessed in Mexico, for instance, does not evoke great confidence. The principal issues of concern for the studies were therefore related to sustainability and the social and economic benefits that can accrue to communities within which telecentres are situated. The studies addressed four major issues:

- Access
- Relevance
- Sustainability (ownership, management, etc.)
- Environments (technological, social, economic, and political).

Research questions

The major research questions addressed by the study were the following (see Appendix II):

- What is the nature of access to ICTs within the telecentres?
- How relevant (i.e., useful and appropriate) are the services and content offered or available at the telecentres to community members and how well do they meet community needs?
- What economic, infrastructure, social, educational, or political factors contribute to, or are important to, the sustainability of telecentres?
- What is the nature of the social, economic, political, and technological context within which the telecentres operate?

Methodology

The studies used a robust methodology that included both qualitative and quantitative methods to collect rich data from actual and potential telecentre users in the communities. These methods included focus group discussions, naturalistic or realistic observations, in-depth case histories and key-informant interviews, user interviews, document analysis, and photo documentation (see Appendix III).

Sample

The primary sample consisted of the telecentres themselves whereas the secondary samples included respondents. The population from which the primary sample was selected included telecentres in Senegal, Mali, Uganda, Mozambique, and South Africa. A proportion of the IDRC-funded telecentres in the five countries, some jointly funded (ITU–UNESCO–IDRC) telecentres in Uganda and Mali, and some private cybercafés or phone shops were included. This mix was important for the sake of making comparisons and for ensuring that a variety of experiences and models were captured. The criteria used for selecting the telecentre sample included: a location that included both rural and urban telecentres, ownership type, services offered, and telecentre maturity. Telecentres that had been operating for less than 12 months were not investigated. Thirty-six telecentres and cybercafés were involved in the studies (5 in Uganda, 3 in Mali, 2 in Mozambique, 6 in South Africa, and 20 in Senegal).

The survey samples were drawn from the population of the catchment area around each of the telecentres, that is, the actual population of users and "potential users" of the telecentres constituted the sample. The total number of individuals who provided information was 3,586.

Instruments

A number of different instrument types were used to capture the rich variety of information. These included a telecentre layout and usage observation guide, a focus group discussion guide, a document analysis guide, an individual case-study interview schedule, a key-informant interview schedule, a user exit-interview schedule (exit poll), and an individual questionnaire. In Mali and Senegal, in addition to the individual questionnaire, an organizational questionnaire was also administered.

Key concepts

IT or ICT

The acronyms 'IT' and 'ICT' are commonly used in contemporary discussions of computers and computer-based communication and information technology. The term 'IT' (information technology), which entered the lexicon earlier, appears to have been overtaken by a preference for its new relative 'ICT' (information and communication technology). The usage of the acronym 'IT' now appears to be restricted to the more technical components or elements of the subject matter.

What are ICTs?

Generally speaking, ICTs include all those instruments, modes, and means both old and new through which information and or data are transmitted or communicated from one person to another or from place to place. Listed among ICTs are: the telephone, facsimile, video, television, radio, print material (e.g., newspapers and books), and computer-based or computer-mediated modes (e.g., email, chat and news groups, list-serves, electronic conferencing, CD-ROMs, etc.). Even early technologies for communicating information, such as the talking drum ought rightly to belong on this list. Increasingly however, when ICTs are discussed, the notion is of computer-mediated forms and modes, yet these are only the newest ones. A reality, fast gaining prominence and power is that of convergence meaning a combination of IC technologies or formats for delivering information and communication. This is manifest in the complexity in the capacities of new generation mobile phones for example which have audio, print and video outputs or services. To a certain extent the telecentre concept operates on the basis of functional convergence.

What is a telecentre?

A telecentre is an integrated information and communication facility that houses a combination of both new and not-so new ICTs (e.g., television, video, facsimile, telephone, computers with Internet connectivity, and sometimes books). This type of facility in which a number of different information and communication technologies are housed and used in an integrated manner is seen as the modern telecentre and is called a multipurpose telecentre. There is, however, a certain variety in the form, facilities, and functions available at telecentres, from the simple telecentre with only one or two telephones and no link to the World Wide Web, to a centre with numerous telephones, facsimile machines, printers, and computers connected to the Internet. Telecentres provide public access to communication and information for economic, social and cultural development or telecommunication and information services for a range of developmental aims. The notion of universal access, which is based on Article 19 of the "Universal Declaration of Human Rights" has provided fodder for the expansion of information and communication services to all without discrimination. Telecentres are seen as potent instruments in the struggle for universal access especially in poor countries and environments.

The nomenclature of telecentres is coloured by differences in geography, purpose etc. Telecentres are also known as Public Access Points and a large number of other names: *Telecentre, telecottage, telekiosk, teleboutique, phone shop, infocentre, telehaus, telestugen, digital clubhouse, cabinas puiblicas, multi-purpose access centre, community technology centre, (CTC), multi-purpose community telecentre (MCT), community access centre, multi-purpose community centre (MPCC), community media centre (CMC)* or *community learning centre (CLC), community multi-media centre, electronic village hall, tele-village or cybercafé,* and the list goes on.

Ownership and management patterns in addition to primary purpose also confer other layers of differentiation on telecentres and on the taxonomy. Simple telecentres are popular in Senegal, whereas multipurpose (community) telecentres are a recent creation of development agencies and, although their financial sustainability is an ongoing concern, their validity and utility have become firmly rooted. To date the telecentre idea has been generally adopted in the United States, Canada and Australia, whereas in Africa and Asia the notion is still only taking root having commenced in the latter half of the 1990s.

What is Schoolnet?

The term 'Schoolnet' is a shortened version of 'school networking'. School networking is the electronic connection of schools and students for purposes of enhancing teaching and learning. The physical facility and organizational entity that builds and maintains this connection is what is referred to as a Schoolnet. There are currently efforts to start Schoolnets in many African countries and there is a continental version called Schoolnet Africa, currently located in South Africa.

Structure

The eight chapters in this book comprise three broad sections; the introduction, findings and conclusions. Chapters 1 and 2, which constitute the introductory section, provide the institutional and continental contexts as well as the rationale for the studies and projects whose findings form the bulk of the book. While chapter 1 introduces Acacia, the programme initiative within the International Development Research Centre charged with the responsibility for ICTs, chapter 2 attempts to place Africa on the global ICT landscape. Chapters 3–7 provide details of the country case studies, with each chapter devoted to one country. Chapter 3 describes findings from the Timbuktu telecentre in Mali and showcases the benefits of partnership between international development agencies and a national telecommunications company with technical expertise and political support in a materially well-resourced and technically competent facility. The utility of multi-donor collaboration is sharply sculpted by findings reported in chapter 4, which show that despite operating in a particularly challenging environment, the Mozambique telecentres made good with comparatively less financial and technical support in comparison with the case in Mali. In Uganda, the tale as narrated in chapter 5 is like one of three cities with findings from telecentres that mirror the conditions of Timbuktu, and Mozambique's Manhiça and Namaacha as well as private experience. Chapter 5 therefore provides the reader with pictures that allow useful comparisons. Chapters 6 (South Africa) and 7 (Senegal) show glimpses from a large number of telecentres, which suggest that telecentre mushrooming is a reality, although failure and collapse are ever-present. In chapter 8, using the research questions as organizing nodes, a summary of key findings is given. The chapter concludes with the notion that the telecentre, like the school or the health centre, which came before, is here to stay.

Chapter 2

ICTs in Africa: The landscape for growing telecentres

Introduction

It is indisputable that advances in microelectronics and telecommunications in conjunction with the results of convergence of the technologies with the resultant new information and communication technologies, during the final quarter of the last century have transformed the way the world works. This transformation is unparalleled since the industrial revolution. This new revolution, the technology revolution, has the added quality of driving change at a much faster pace. It took almost five hundred years for the steam engine to spread throughout the world, whereas the Internet, developed in the 1970s, has reached all the continents and is still spreading fast. In 1996 only five African countries had Internet capability, today all are connected and internet-enabled. This new age variously labelled the computer, Internet, or information age commoditizes knowledge ensuring that the information and knowledge rich are also rich by other more conventional measures. This has translated into a divide whose contours appear to trace earlier demarcations of rich and poor societies, of developed and developing countries.

The information revolution of the late twentieth century has introduced significant changes in the nature of human interactions and relations between peoples and nations. One word that epitomizes the nature of the change wrought by the new order is globalization. Globalization is a contemporary global pre-occupation and its pre-eminent vehicle, information and communication technologies. Globalization is resulting in integrated world markets as never before and we are reminded frequently that those nations which remain un-integrated will fail to derive the benefits of large scale and international trade or the other benefits of the new information and communication technologies. While most developed countries are well on their way to fully integrating the new technologies, developing countries, and Africa in particular, are much further behind in adopting their use. The result of this differential adoption is the digital divide.

Sub-Saharan Africa and South Asia are at the bottom of the list of world regions in digital prosperity and opportunity. On account they are currently receiving considerable attention from the contemporary global preoccupation with bridging the digital divide. The widespread and high-level engagement with the digital divide does not stem primarily from benign good neighbourliness but from calculated interests addressed at reaping the handsome benefits of digital opportunities wherever these may be found. It is said on one hand that the less ICT developed countries are not able to participate effectively in the accelerated process of globalization and acceleration of growth and transformation of work and factors of production now occurring as a result of these tools. On the other hand, the ICT developed countries cannot effectively and efficiently globalize capitalist expansion into new and emerging markets without a minimum existence of the requisite ICT tools.

The entire world economic system is undergoing changes. Work structures, systems and organizations are being transformed. New economic dynamics of space and time in relation to work are emerging. Global competition and globalizing business, now the norm, means that international capital is likely to go to countries that have the facilities and tools needed for the modern economy. New opportunities for creating wealth and economic growth through ICTs have been demonstrated in countries able to take advantage of their potential. ICTs are also widely believed to be useful in the positive transformation of governance as they improve the opportunities and capability of individuals and marginalized groups to participate in the process. Although the penetration and use of ICTs is still very low in the African continent in comparison to more developed countries, a number of examples currently exist of how ICTs are being exploited and deployed to improve the lives and livelihoods of Africans (see examples of novel ICT use).

Encouraging as these developments are, there are still too few of these examples largely because of the poor communication infrastructure, the low level of ICT penetration and the limits imposed by weak supporting environments necessary for the effective use of ICTs in Africa.

The remainder of this chapter provides some more detail of the context of the more widespread ICTs within which initiatives geared towards improving access have grown and concludes with a look at telecentres as the new public information access points.

Examples of novel ICT use

- A local Internet service provider in Morocco has a contract to digitize the National Library of France's paper archives. The documents are scanned in France, sent by satellite link to Morocco, and edited by keyboard operators in Rabat.
- In Togo and Mauritius, call centres now provide telephone support services for international companies with customers in Europe and North America. Callers do not realize they are calling Mauritius or Togo. They pick up the phone, dial a local number, and are routed to one of these countries where the operators provide the support that they require.
- In Cape Verde 'virtual security guards' have jobs using the Internet to monitor web cams in office parks on the east coast of the United States. They notify local rapid response teams in the US if they see anything amiss.
- Many African craft makers are selling their wares on the world-wide-web, supported by NGOs such as PeopleLink.
- The government of Lesotho recently declared that all announcements for cabinet and committee meetings would be made only be email.
- Some governments, such as those in South Africa, Algeria, and Tunisia, now provide immediate global access to tender offers via the Internet.
- In South Africa, the results of blood tests are being transmitted to remote clinics that are not connected to the national telecommunications grid via mobile telephone text messages.
- In Uganda a local women's organization the Council for the Economic Empowerment of Women in Africa (CEEWA) posts prices and market information for agricultural commodities regularly on its web site and women in rural trading centres can access this information at a number of community telecentres to determine which market to take their wares and what to charge for them.
- In Senegal local fishing communities are using Personal Digital Assistants to improve distribution and marketing of their products and improving their incomes.

ICTs in Africa: Context and background

The continental ICT landscape has changed dramatically since the last decade of the 1990s. Much of this change, instigated by international action and contained in multilateral agreements has been geared towards creating spaces for global international capital. Quite often, international development action follows the trends and directions established by the conventions and treaties. Much of the recent ICT activity and activism as was the case with the radio and television (mass media) in the 1960s, has been bolstered by external support.

Broadcasting

Television and radio broadcasting are widely available. However, radio is by far the most dominant mass communication instrument or medium in Africa. Ownership of radio sets is far higher than for any other electronic device. It is estimated for example that in 1997 radio ownership in Africa was close to 170 million and growing at a rate of 4% per annum. The estimate for 2002 was over 200 million radio sets. The corresponding figure for television sets is put at 62 million. It is estimated that over 60% of the population of the sub-continent is reached by existing radio networks whereas national television coverage is largely confined to the major towns. Some countries still do not have national television broadcasting stations and even relatively well-resourced Botswana only launched its national television broadcasting station in 2002.

The number of commercial and community radio stations is steadily increasing following liberalization of the broadcast sector in many countries. But, a large portion of the news and information output is often rebroadcast from either national (state-owned/operated) broadcast news, or international broadcast news from agencies such as Voice of America, the BBC or Radio France International.

Satellite-based broadcasting has seen a major boost in activity on the continent in the last few years. In 1995, the South African company M-Net launched the world's first digital direct-to-home subscriber satellite service called DSTV. Subscribers have access to over 30 video channels and 40 audio programmes on C-band to the whole of Africa and on lower-cost Ku-band to Southern Africa, south of Lusaka. In 2001, the South African Broadcasting Corporation (SABC) the national broadcaster launched

Channel Africa, a new satellite-based continent-wide news and entertainment channel. In 1998, WorldSpace, a United States-based company launched a commercial digital radio broadcasting satellite called AfriStar to which broadcasters in Europe, the United States, Egypt, Burkina Faso, Kenya, Mali, Senegal, and South Africa have signed up. WorldSpace aims to make over 80 audio channels available to listeners on the continent who can afford the 50 or so US dollars to purchase the special digital receiver.

Community radio broadcasting has had a slow take-off and local community broadcast stations are still few with Ghana, Mali, South Africa, and Uganda being the exceptions with a number of new community radio licensees. There is also a growing interest in transforming community telecentres or at the very least linking them with community radio stations as the ultimate information convergence scheme using the same facilities to access the Internet, and for better radio programming. This project is however still very much in its infancy.

Telecommunications

There have been significant changes in the telecommunications sector in Africa in the recent past. These changes have been on three broad fronts. There have been policy changes, institutional innovations, as well as technical and operational changes all of which have been catalysed by new liberalization and privatisation regimes. Partly on account of these a substantial increase in the rate of expansion and modernization of fixed line (terrestrial) networks is taking place, accompanied by an explosion in mobile networks and satellite-based telecommunication services.

The number of fixed lines grew at about 9% annually between 1995 and 2001. The sub-Saharan Africa (excluding South Africa) fixed-line teledensity in 2001 was one per 130 inhabitants. Taking into account population growth, the effective annual increase in lines is therefore only 6%. Most of the existing telecommunications infrastructure does not reach the majority of the population because most of the available capacity is concentrated in capital cities. In some 15 African countries (more than 70% of the fixed lines are still located in the largest city (ITU, 2002). Between 1995 and 2001 the number of fixed lines nearly doubled increasing from 12.5 million to 21 million across Africa. Much of this growth took place in North and South Africa with the former having 11.4 million lines and South Africa, 5 million. Sub-Saharan Africa, with about 10% of the world's population (626 million), currently has only 0.2% of the world's 1 billion telephone lines. When compared with other low-income countries (all of which house 40% of the world's population and 10% of the telephone lines), the telephone penetration on the subcontinent is about five times worse than the "average" low-income country.

Although telecommunications infrastructure is beginning to spread, domestic use has until recently been largely confined to a small elite that can afford the high cost of owning a telephone. There are huge variations between countries in installation charges, line rental, and call tariffs. ITU figures reported for 2002 show that for an average-size business in Africa installation costs over USD 100, rental, USD 6 a month, and USD 0.11 for a 3-minute local call. In some countries e.g., Egypt, Benin, Mauritania, Niger, and Togo, installation charges exceed USD 200 while line rentals range from USD 0.8 to USD 20 a month, and call charges vary by a factor of 10; from USD 0.60 an hour to over USD 5 an hour. Thus on average the cost of renting a connection on the continent is almost 20% of GDP per capita, as opposed to a world average of 9% and 1% in high-income countries. Public telephones do not compensate for the high cost of maintaining private telephone connections by being ubiquitous. On the contrary, the numbers are still much lower than in other parts of the world. In 2001 there were about 350,000 public telephones in the entire continent, 75,000 of these in sub-Saharan Africa (about 1 for every 8,500 people), compared with a world average of 1 for every 500 people and a high-income country average of 1 for every 200 people.

The most dramatic changes in the telecommunications landscape in the last decade of the second millennium have been witnessed with mobile telephone networks. Mobile phone subscribers now outnumber fixed-line users in most countries and with numbers reaching a total of 24 million subscriptions in 2001, this uptake demonstrates the unmet need for basic voice services, which state-run fixed network operators have been unable to fulfil in their long years of monopoly. On account of relatively lower costs and long-range cellular base stations, many rural areas have also benefited from mobile coverage. These developments and a number of new communication products have been catalysed by the growing satellite coverage over the continent.

A growing phenomenon is for governments to thrust some of the responsibility for providing public telephony to the private sector through franchises and other arrangements. This partly explains the rapid growth of public 'phone shops' and 'teleboutiques' in many countries. The best-known example is in Senegal, which has over 10,000 commercially run public telephone bureaus popularly called telecentres, which employ more than 15,000 people and generate a sizeable chunk of national revenues. Although most of the telecentres are in urban areas, many are being established in remote rural locations. Some telecentres are now providing Internet access and other more advanced ICT services.

In rural areas, which usually lie outside the fixed (grid) infrastructure, the numbers of public call centres using mobile networks to provide services are growing, but the cost of mobile services is prohibitive for most rural folk. At about USD 0.50 per minute on average, regular telephone calls or Internet access is too expensive for them. One reason for the high cost of mobile telephony is related to interconnection. Mobile networks usually depend on the terrestrial telecommunication infrastructure that is often owned and controlled by the premier telecom (usually the national incumbent) for call termination. This dependence translates into financial relations with the incumbent telecom and this is ultimately reflected in call and user charges. Currently, interconnection is a big issue across the continent as mobile operators and terrestrial service providers are locked in financial battles over appropriate fees. Even between mobile operators themselves there are also issues of interconnection when calls originate from one network and terminate in another.

In South Africa as in some other countries (e.g., Kenya), licensed mobile operators have Universal Service obligations which make it imperative for them not only to provide services to rural areas but also at subsidized tariffs. This means that while mobile services have a chance of growing in rural areas, fixed line phone shops that cannot compete with the lower GSM tariffs cannot sustain businesses in rural settings. As a result, terrestrial telephony, the base for more advanced (Internet, heavy data transfer) and secure services cannot be nurtured beyond the urban centres. However, SMS gateways to the Internet are now allowing access to limited data such as commodity and market prices and weather reports in some countries such as Uganda and Kenya.

The Internet

Since its creation in the 1970s, the Internet and the products it has spurned, e.g., email have become very powerful tools for information and communication and a commonly used short-hand indicator of a country's level of ICT adoption and integration.

In Africa, the pattern of Internet diffusion has been similar to that of mobile telephone networks. Although not as widespread, the Internet whose introduction preceded the mobile phone made an early foothold and impact at the top end of business, in wealthy families, primarily in the major urban areas. The non-profit sector; academic institutions and NGOs pioneered Internet use in the early 1990s, fuelled by their need for low cost international communications. Private Internet Service Providers (ISPs), and national telecom operators subsequently took it up and seem to be dominating the field currently. Table 2 shows that sub-Saharan Africa's Internet use grew between 1998 and 2000 but at a slower rate than other parts of the world. Sub-Saharan Africa along with South Asia, are located at the bottom of the scale in worldwide Internet usage.

Table 2. Internet users as percentage of total population

Region	1998	2000
United States	26.3	54.3
High-income OECD (excluding US)	6.9	28.2
Latin America and the Caribbean	0.8	3.2
East Asia and the Pacific	0.5	2.3
Eastern Europe and CIS	0.8	3.9
Arab States	0.2	0.6
Sub-Saharan Africa	0.1	0.4
South Asia	0.04	0.4
World	2.4	6.7

Source: UNDP *World Development Report 2001*.

Arguments abound in respect of the true value of an indicator such as Internet subscriber-ship as a reflection of the number of users on account of the ubiquity of shared, dormant and unused or unusable accounts. The relatively high and rapidly growing use of public access services such as cybercafés and telecentres, make it genuinely difficult to measure the total number of Internet users in Africa. Although the number of dialup subscriber accounts is readily available, these figures are only a partial gauge of the size of the Internet sector and should be examined together with other factors such as the quantity of international traffic from each country, and the available national bandwidth.

The phenomenal growth of Internet use seen in the 1990s has slowed in most countries. Almost all African capital cities and some secondary towns currently have points of presence (POPs). About 280 are scattered in different locations across the continent. Some argue that the slow down is because the bulk of the users who can afford a computer and telephone have already obtained connections. As of mid-2002, the number of dialup Internet subscribers was close to 1.7 million, 20% up from 2001, bolstered mainly by growth in a few countries such as Nigeria. Of these subscribers, North Africa and South Africa between them are responsible for about 1.2 million, leaving about 500,000 for the other 49 sub-Saharan African countries. If we assume that each computer with an Internet or email connection supports a range of three to five users, this puts current estimates of the number of African Internet users at about 5 to 8 million.

Currently, the average total cost of using a local dialup Internet account for 20 hours a month in Africa is about USD 60 per month (usage fees and local call telephone time included, but not telephone line rental). ISP subscription charges vary between USD 10 and USD 80 a month. The charges are higher than those in the USA or Europe and the charge of 60 USD per month is high for the average monthly income of say a middle-level professional in the public sector in Africa. Twenty hours of Internet access including telephone charges in the United States cost USD 22 per month in 2000, in Germany; USD 33, and across the European Union; USD 39. The per capita incomes in these countries are much higher than in Africa sometimes 10 times greater than the African average. This state of affairs is a reflection of the imperfect nature of the interactions between market forces and government monopolies, which in turn reflect the levels of maturity in markets, the different regulations guiding data transmission services and varying tariff policies.

As a way of improving Internet use, some countries have instituted local call charges for calls to the Internet regardless of distance. This greatly reduces costs for those in remote areas and increases the viability of Internet services provided by rural telecentres. Nineteen countries have adopted this strategy to date: Benin, Burkina Faso, Cape Verde, Chad, Ethiopia,

Gabon, Malawi, Mali, Mauritius, Mauritania, Morocco, Namibia, Niger, Senegal, South Africa, Togo, Tunisia, Uganda, and Zimbabwe. In the Seychelles Internet charges are 50% of the normal rate of local voice calls

But most rural users (and telecentres) still have to make costly long distance calls to connect to the Internet. The high cost of Internet use limits individual use, and creates demand for public telecentres where the cost of a single telephone line (account) can be shared among a host of customers who would not otherwise be able to afford access. Telecentres, cybercafés, telekiosks, etc., address the low-income levels of users by sharing the cost and maintenance of equipment and connectivity amongst a larger number of users. Lower-cost email-only services and free web-based services such as Hotmail, Yahoo, or Excite are very popular. A number of African ISPs such as Africa Online and Mail Africa have set up their own low-cost web-based email services in response.

Internet-based content and applications continue to expand, albeit at a slow rate, and there is still too little attractive, practical or relevant content or easily available applications for the average African Internet user. There are a handful of official general government web sites, such as those of Angola, Egypt, Gabon, Lesotho, Mauritius, Morocco, Mozambique, Senegal, South Africa, Togo, Tunisia, and Zambia, but there is very little government use of the Internet for administrative purposes. Web content is higher in some sectors, e.g., tourism, foreign investment and current affairs. In 1999, the Columbia University African Studies Department identified over 120 different newspapers and news magazines available on the Internet, published in 23 countries. The countries best represented included Côte d'Ivoire, Egypt, Ghana, Kenya, Senegal, South Africa, Tanzania, Zambia, and Zimbabwe.

Outside of South Africa and perhaps a couple of others, few organizations are using the web to deliver significant quantities of information or carry out transactions. Although large numbers of organizations now have a "brochure" website with basic descriptive and contact information, very few actually use the Internet for real business activities. The limited number of nationals with access to the Internet or actively using it for conducting common everyday business is still small. This is aggravated by the widespread absence and use of credit cards, limited skills and expertise for digitizing and coding pages, and the high costs of local web-hosting services. Universal smart card and e-commerce policies are receiving attention in a number of countries as one way to deal with the situation. Mauritius and South Africa are looking at a single smart card that will allow the public to hold drivers' licence data, small amounts of funds for light transactions, and health and other social security information.

ICT equipment and other contextual factors

Recent estimates for the number of personal computers in Africa put the total at about 7.5 million for 2001 – an average of about 1 per 100 people. But due to limited capacity for industry monitoring and the large numbers of machines smuggled in to avoid taxes and import duties, the figures are notoriously unreliable. Official figures may be overestimated by up to three to six times, in which case the average ratio of computers to people could be close to 1 to 500. It is common practice to find multiple users for a single computer..

Underutilization of existing computer resources is also common, often caused by the preponderance of many stand-alone computers in the same office with no use of Local Area Networks (LANs or WANs). Offices quite often have many PCs, but only one is usually fitted with a modem connected to the Internet.

The high cost of computer hardware and software licensing is a major hurdle. As a result increasing attention is being directed toward the use of recycled PCs, thin client solutions, set-top boxes, and other low-cost 'appliances', and applications, Open Source and free software. As if the high purchasing costs are not bad enough, many national tax regimes still treat computers, communications equipment, peripherals and cellular phones as luxury items. Since they are so categorized and because they are almost exclusively imported, duties and taxes on them are very high. This adds to their retail price making them doubly expensive. Although there have been notable efforts in some countries, e.g., Uganda, to reduce or remove import duties on computers, levies are still commonly charged and often at high rates. In some cases international development assistance projects are to import equipment duty-free but this is not standard practice and a number of ICT projects have experienced long delays as a result of matters related to unresolved taxes or duties on equipment.

Other factors also colour the landscape and influence the degree of success that ICT projects can achieve. Of supreme importance is electricity. Electricity drives ICTs yet irregular or nonexistent electricity supplies are a common feature and a major problem in Africa, especially outside the major towns. Many countries have extremely limited power distribution networks that do not penetrate significantly into rural areas. Although substantial improvements have taken place over the last few years, power cuts (regular scheduled power outages for many hours) are still common occurrences, even in capital cities (Accra, Dar-es-Salaam, and Lagos). Like electricity, road, rail, and air transport networks are poorly developed, costly to use, and often in bad condition, resulting in barriers to the movement of people and goods. These networks are critical for the development and maintenance of ICT infrastructure – telephone lines, communications networks etc.

A big headache is the generally low level of education and literacy, especially scientific and technical literacy among the population, which has created a great scarcity of technical skills and expertise at all levels. This is compounded by the very low pay scales in the African civil service that are a chronic problem for governments and NGOs, and guarantee the continual loss of the brightest and most experienced IT technicians to the private sector and in some instances to more developed countries in a never ending stream of 'brain drain'. Rural areas in particular suffer similarly as most enterprising skilled technicians find better jobs in the big cities.

Finally, the policies and business climate of the ICT sector in Africa, suffer from well-known ailments: small markets divided by arbitrary borders, non-transparent and time-consuming business registration and licensing procedures, limited opportunities (due largely to the historic pattern of monopolies and high levels of state control), scarce local capital, currency instability, exchange controls and inflation.

Some of the contextual issues are currently being addressed by a number of efforts and proposals. The African Information Society Initiative (AISI) and the New Partnership for African Development (NEPAD) come readily to mind. The AISI is a framework for the formulation and development of national information and communication infrastructure (NICI) to address national development priorities in every African country, which simultaneously calls for cooperation among African countries in the sharing of experiences, expertise and resources. With support from the UNECA and a number of other international organizations many countries have commenced the articulation and implementation of national NICI plans, and 17 countries have finalized their strategies: Benin, Burkina Faso, Cape Verde, Côte d'Ivoire, Egypt, Gambia, Mauritania, Mauritius, Morocco, Mozambique, Rwanda, Senegal, Seychelles, South Africa, Sudan, and Tunisia. High on the list of priorities in many of the countries is improvement of access to ICTs in rural areas through the use of public access points popularly called telecentres.

Toward universal service: Telecentres and public access

Efforts to promote universal access to ICTs in Africa have been on the agenda of meetings of high-level policymakers since the early 1990s. An important watershed in the maturation of the idea of universal access and of the emergence of community telecentres is the first World Telecommunications Development Conference in 1994, which produced the Buenos Aires declaration. Further official recognition was given to the issue in 1996 when the Conference of African Ministers of Social and Economic Planning requested the UN Economic Commission for Africa to set up a 'high-level working group' to chart Africa's path to the global information highway. The result was the framework document that created the African Information Society Initiative (AISI), which was adopted by Ministers of Planning. Since this historic beginning, communications ministers from over 40 African countries have endorsed the AISI and AISI activities are still continuing. One area of priority action in the AISI engendered NICI plans is the improvement of access to ICTs usually referred to as Universal access in rural areas for which telecentres are a recent strategy.

The telecentre concept has since received considerable attention and support from the international development community, a number of national governments, public telecom operators as well as private telecom service providers. This attention has translated into many pilot telecentre projects scattered across the developing world. Over 20 projects have been implemented in Ghana, Mozambique, Uganda, Benin, South Africa, Tanzania, Zambia, and Zimbabwe. Along with the IDRC, which produced one of the first studies of telecentres (Fuchs 1997), many development agencies are active in this area including the British Council, CDG, CTA, FAO, IICD, ITU, UNDP, UNESCO, the World Bank, and USAID.

Definition and development of telecentres

Nomenclature

The telecentre idea was born less than twenty years ago in 1985 in Velmdalen a small farming village in Sweden. The concept is recognised and called by a large number of very different names. There is little doubt that the names by which the telecentre is known will change (grow or shrink who can tell?) as the movement matures and globalizes. To date the idea has been generally adopted in the United States, Canada and Australia. In Africa and Asia the notion is still taking root.

Taxonomy

As indicated in chapter 1, the form and functions of the various facilities subsumed under the umbrella notion of telecentre vary. This is understandable and in some way to be expected. The telecentre is a phenomenon still in discovery and in the various places where it is created, the local context colours its final form. It is an instrument for development whose adaptation and mutation is far from complete and perhaps not for some time yet. As a result, attempts to classify the currently existing types are still quite unsophisticated.

Gomez et al (1999b) identify five types of telecentres:

- **Basic telecentre**, usually located in rural marginalized areas where there is limited access to basic services in general where training of potential users is a popular service in addition to internet access.
- **Telecentre franchise,** a series of independently owned and managed interconnected telecentres usually supervised by a local organization, which offers technical and on occasion, financial support.
- **Civil telecentre**, usually the most common, where a public organization such as a university opens up its facilities like computers for use by the public and the telecentre services tend to be an addition to the other day to day activities of the organization.
- **Cybercafé**, commercial in nature and found in affluent neighbourhoods or hotels and in major towns and cities; and
- **The multi purpose community centre**, one of the newer models recently introduced in a number of countries offering more specialised services such as tele-medicine.

The difficulty with the classification by Gomez et al is that the distinguishing criteria are mixed and the logic hard to comprehend. In one instance it is based on location (cybercafé), in the next, on the nature of ownership (civil telecentre) and in another, on the type of services offered (basic telecentre). The classification attempted by Collee and Roman (1999) shows the complexity and identify the dimensions that any taxonomy would do well to

consider.
On the basis of their classification (Collee and Roman 1999), it is possible to distinguish the following telecentre types:

- Public/private
- Publicly or privately funded
- Commercial (fee-based)/free
- Urban/rural
- Narrow-focus/multi-purpose
- Independent/networked, grouped
- Community/establishment-based
- Stand alone/attached
- Profit/service
- Thematic/universal

There still appears to be work before we arrive at a satisfactory and exhaustive classification of telecentres. Like the naming and grouping of telecentres, the nature of the development and evolution of these facilities is still being theorized.

Evolution of telecentres

While there appears to be a general consensus about the basic function of telecentres, there is a debate around the nature of optimal ownership, management and operations. Fuchs (1997), for instance, suggests the function of telecentres to be the provision of "public access to communication and information for economic, social and cultural development..." and Zongo (1999) concurring states that the telecentre "provides telecommunication and information services for a range of developmental aims".

It has been suggested that the ownership, management and operations evolve over time and three stages have been described. Fuchs (1997), identified the investment, contract and user fee stages.

- The **investment stage** is seen as characterizing the early state where a non-profit making organization forms a partnership with a local community in an attempt to build community capacity through encouraging them to participate in the information society. At this stage the organization finances the information technology initiatives, provides

equipment and training for local partners, key persons and staff, as a way of demonstrating practical utility.
- In the **contract stage** the telecentre has gained autonomy from the "parent" organizations and starts to make contractual agreements with other agencies such as government departments or other organizations, e.g., hospitals or schools building up a clientele to which it provides services as well as technical support in the setting up of their facilities.
- By the time the telecentre gets to the **user fee stage** donor dependency is a thing of the past, since by this time the communities are well aware of the products and benefits of the telecentre and are therefore willing to pay for services.

The implication of an evolutionary view is that it is only a matter of time and maturity before telecentres become independent and self-sustaining or sustainable. There is however some difficulty with this position. The evolutionary thesis, gives slight attention to motivational issues and the wide variety of telecentres, and appears to pertain more to one type of telecentre; the public development-oriented telecentre. To be fair, these were the types investigated by Fuchs. The preoccupation with sustainability and economic independence of this particular type of telecentre has continued to dominate discussions partly on account of the current insistence on market logic and the business model. Yet few examples of telecentres at the **user fee stage** have been described in the literature and this is perhaps proof that not enough time has elapsed for the evolution to advance to this stage or that other conceptual and theoretical models need to be constructed to explain and account for the full spectrum of experiences. On the other hand, the reality of many failed telecentres underscores the importance of economic viability. How to achieve this remains a big question. Other questions also abound.

Glimpses from the literature

Despite the recency of the movement and the relative paucity of telecentre research, or perhaps on account of it, a number of unresolved and pertinent issues emerge in the available literature. Careful reading of the literature suggests that sustainability is multidimensional and dependent on more than just the availability of financial resources. Factors commonly associated with sustainability include the operating environment, ownership and management styles, community participation, relevance of services and content. The logic of the market seems to place great premium on what in the literature is referred to as access – numbers of users and types of usage. The political rationale for the entire telecentre movement is predicated on this Universal Access criterion. The notion of universal access, which can be traced to the Universal Declaration of Human Rights and Article 19 in particular provided the fodder for the expansion of information and communication services to all without discrimination. Telecentres are seen as instruments in the battle for universal access especially in poor countries and environments. Data pictures from telecentres suggest that access is still limited, i.e., not available to all and some groups are favoured while others are marginalized. Women have been shown to be particularly vulnerable (Karelse and Sylla 2000; Rathgeber 2000, 2002; Hafkin 2002). Use is most pronounced among young educated men (Kyabwe and Kibombo 1999). The literature points to several factors that affect access directly and indirectly. Foremost is cost. The high cost of establishing the facilities and maintaining the services means that there cannot be nearly as any as there ought to be to cater for the extent of demand. The start-up cost of telecentres in South Africa is said to be as high as USD 40,000 (Benjamin and Dahms 1999). Grants for two-year projects can be anywhere between USD100,000 and USD500,000, depending on the types and numbers of equipment. Operating costs were often overlooked in early projects (Delgadillo and Borja 1999).

The cost of use (user fees/charges) for potential clients is also a significant hurdle. Telecentres usually charge user fees and although these are often low and subsidized, there is the feeling that the fees are high for poor people with little disposable incomes – women and younger people in general. Another aspect, which directly affects access and use, is the location of the telecentre. Like schools and hospitals in colonial towns as opposed to traditional markets, telecentres that are not carefully sited have been shown to draw fewer customers (Kyabwe and Kibombo 1999) on account of physical inaccessibility. In addition to the location, the physical layout/ plan, and the psychological accessibility of the telecentre have been shown to influence patronage. Some users value privacy, which is not always guaranteed in telecentres and the power of psychological dimensions of use, has been pointed out (Baron 1999; Harris 1999; Cisler et al 1999).

The language used in the telecentre is as important as the cost of services, if not more, for access. The language of operations and the language of services, i.e., language of the content and the holdings (books, websites, videos, manuals, etc) are very important. It has been suggested that English language (the language of ICTs) is often a barrier to learning about new technologies in contexts where most people are either non-literate or semi-illiterate (Dandar 1999; Delgadillo and Borja 1999). Other than acting as a barrier to comprehension and ultimately social change, the language question also borders on relevance. Taking account of the low levels of English language literacy and the ubiquity of vernacular in the rural locations, the relevance of material in English language is highly questionable.

Other factors, which affect the success of telecentres highlighted in the literature, are operative at the micro and macro socio-political levels and include such aspects as the national policy environment and local social arrangements for the control and management of facilities. In the late 1990s the move to create new policy instruments that would support growth in the sector on a continent-wide scale commenced with the Africa Information Society Initiative and Africa Development Forum. The moderate harvest of new National Information and Communication Infrastructure plans or ICT policies in about a third of the countries is testimony that things are indeed changing. At the level of the telecentres themselves management and local community involvement appear to have some influence on telecentre outcomes and fortunes. Sound management and high level community support are prescribed for success yet in places community involvement may be disruptive if and when community members active in the facility have different or hidden agendas. Community ownership is also believed to be related to success but models of true ownership are rare since most community telecentres are not genuinely owned or completely administered by the communities.

Conclusion

Although the telecentre movement and its study is still in infancy, available research sheds light on some of the issues while pointing directions for further research and theory building to guide the practical implementation and establishment of more telecentres. Menou (1999) and Gomez et al (1999) suggest that the search for parameters, indicators and tools to assess the impact of ICTs for development is a long way from complete. But perhaps most urgently required is a robust theory that explains the relationship between telecentres and development (Heeks 2002). The urgency is intoned to avoid the mis-application of a potentially powerful tool as the world appears poised to implement a massive roll-out and adoption of ICTs in this century.

Chapter 3

Timbuktu Telecentre, Mali

Located in West Africa, Mali is a country with a rich history and culture, although its entry into the twenty-first century has been slow and limited. Among the poorest countries in the world with a GDP of USD230 per capita, Mali has low levels of literacy and participation in formal education. Factors such as these have played a major role in keeping the majority of Malians out of the technological age. Women as a group are particularly disadvantaged. In 1995, the adult literacy rate for men was 39%; whereas, that for women was 29%. In the same vein, the net primary enrolment ratio for girls was 33% and for boys 47% (UNICEF WCARO 2001).

This chapter presents the results of a study conducted in Mali between December 2000 and February 2001. The sample of 135 individuals included users, potential users, community leaders, and heads of local organizations and government departments. In addition to the Timbuktu MCT, two private telephone booths and one cybercafé in the city were also investigated.

Telecommunications context

Mali has an ICT policy that is based on the principles of bringing information technology and communications services closer to the people and of reducing costs to guarantee access to all. The policy enacted in February 2000 when President Alpha Konaré organized the Bamako 2000 ICT forum became operational in May 2001 with the creation of the ICT Commission based in the Prime Minister's office. Since then, a massive connection project has been started to link 703 rural communes based on the experience of the Timbuktu MCT pilot.

By early 2001, Mali was one of sixteen African countries with local dialup Internet access nationwide. The national telecommunications operator

(SOTELMA) created a strategy for the provision of local telephone and Internet access across the country and introduced special 'area-codes' to allow Internet access to be charged at local call rates. This allowed Internet providers to create a national network at reduced rates, which has spread to remote areas of the country. In February 2001, there were 31,000 telephone lines serving the entire population of the country, and the number of Internet subscribers was estimated to be 1,000.

Timbuktu

The principal subject of this study is the multipurpose community telecentre (MCT) in Timbuktu. Although three private facilities were also investigated, data analysis and discussion concentrate on the MCT. The Timbuktu telecentre commenced as a joint project of the ITU, UNESCO, and IDRC in 1998. It was one of five on the continent. The others were in Uganda, Benin, Tanzania, and Mozambique, and of these, those in Uganda and Mozambique are also discussed in this book. When the study was undertaken, the projects in Benin and Tanzania were just starting and not included in the sample.

Timbuktu is steeped in history and dates back to the 12th Century. To the north of Timbuktu, a dune system with desolate landscapes heralds the Sahel or Azaouad desert. The area's meagre resources and the harsh climate support only a nomadic existence. The tropical sub-arid climate is characterized by very long dry seasons and a very short and irregular rainy season. Temperatures reach a high of 45° C and a low of 7° C, and rainfall rarely exceeds 200 mm a year.

To the south of Timbuktu, only 18 km away, lies the valley of Issa-Ber, which is endowed with abundant water, is green for most of the year, and bustles with life. It is the centre of cultural activities. Settlements in Issa-Ber are permanent, and people are scattered in small villages dotted along the water sources. The town of Timbuktu is a small dot in the heart of a huge, flat, open country. Although the urban landscape is dotted by houses made of stone or earth, the rural houses are usually straw huts and skin tents.

The juxtaposition of the natural environments of the Sahel and the Issa-Ber are also reflected in the human contrasts. The nomads, the Arab and Berber caravaneers and the Tuareg herders, are quite distinct from the sedentary Songhoi farmers, and from the artisans, the traders, and workers of the informal sector.

Timbuktu has six preschool facilities, sixteen schools for basic education, one vocational training institute (for training teachers for middle and upper basic education schools), four madarassahs (Muslim religious colleges, one of which has a middle and upper school), and thirty Koranic schools. Education is provided in the Sonrai, Tamachèq, and Arabic languages.

The principal economic activities of Timbuktu are trade, agriculture (market gardening), livestock, and arts and craft. The ancient city is a favourite tourist attraction. Timbuktu is also an economic hub as it is the centre of local administration and a crossroads for merchants and citizens residing in Azaouad and on the banks of the Issa-Ber. However, the movement of people and goods is made difficult due to the poor state of the infrastructure. Rural inhabitants often move around on foot, ride on animals (horse, camel, and cattle), or travel in canoes.

Infrastructure and technology in Timbuktu is not as advanced as one would expect for a city of such historical significance. Timbuktu is at the junction of a road network, although river transportation is important during the rainy season when water levels rise. A new airport has made air travel in and out of Timbuktu easier.

Four radio broadcasting stations are located in the vicinity of Timbuktu: El Farouk, Lafia, Bouctou, and Jamana. The telecommunication sector in Timbuktu is characterized by:

- A digital telephone centre that provides for standard and telephone booth usage and some data transmission. The exchange has the capacity for eight telephone booths but only two are equipped and operating; and
- A digital transmission centre that uses a satellite earth station to link Timbuktu with Bamako and 13 districts in the region. Current carrying capacity is 472 subscribers, but there were only 344 subscribers at the time of the study.

Together, these systems support Timbuktu's telecommunications infrastructure, which provides telephony and data transmission on the switched telephone network (PSTN) up to a maximum of 32 Kbits. In January 2001, there were 640 telephone subscribers in Timbuktu and over 400 pending applications for telephone lines. The telecentre was attracting many people on account of the huge level of unmet need and the demand for ICT services.

Findings

Layout and facilities

Initially housed in the premises of the Timbuktu regional hospital between April and October 1999, the telecentre moved to the Town Hall in premises made available free of charge by the municipality. The telecentre is located opposite the Place de l'Indépendance and the regional High Commission, adjacent to the local police station, and 400 m from the Mahamane Haïdara High School in the centre of town. However, the telecentre is in search of ideal premises. The construction of a large building (300 m^2) that was expected to house the telecentre had stalled at the time of the investigation. The premises that are under construction are near the main town road about 500 m from the Town Hall, the current location, and not far from other public utilities.

At the time of the study, the telecentre occupied a total of four rooms. The largest room (25 m^2) was being used as a training and reception area; the second room (24 m^2) was used as the Internet and facsimile office; and the two smaller rooms served as the server room and the manager's office-cum-store. The telecentre did not have enough room to create a waiting room or reception area to accommodate waiting customers. The number of waiting customers often exceeded the number of users, and there was no privacy for telephone users. The telecentre did have new and comfortable furniture, which included six executive desks, five metal tables, ten wooden tables, thirty executive chairs, and twelve plastic chairs. However, the telecentre staff felt the furniture was inadequate.

An inventory of the equipment available at the telecentre (see Table 3) showed that there were fifteen computers, four of which were not being used at the time because they had 'broken down.' The majority of computers were Pentiums. Of the four available 486s, only one was found to be in good working condition. A new monitor was found to be faulty. Other equipment included three printers, one facsimile machine, and one digital camera. Table 3 indicates that most of the equipment was in good working condition and that the telecentre was quite well equipped. The Timbuktu telecentre was better equipped than most of the others telecentres in this study. All the computers were using some version of the Microsoft® Windows operating system (either Windows 95, 98, or 2000). Table 4 lists the software manuals and electronic documents that were available in the Telecentre most of these in French. The number of CD-ROMs is quite limited compared with the amount of hardware.

Table 3. Inventory of telecentre equipment

Equipment	Types	Available	Used	Not used	Reason
Computers					
PC Wave	Pentium II	1	1		
Dell	Pentium II	4	4		
Authentic AMD	Pentium I	4	3	1	Broken down
Laptop Toshiba	Pentium II	1	1		
X86 Family AT	Pentium I	1	1		
PC Express 486	486SX	4	1	3	Broken down
	Total	15	11	4	
Monitors					
Shamrock		1	1		
APT Provista		4	4		
Dell		6	5	1	New but faulty
Other		3	1	2	New in storage
	Total	14	11	3	
Mice					
Microsoft		3	3		
Genius		1	1		
Artec		4	3	1	Not working
Other Equipment					
Printer	HPLaserJet 51	1	1		
Colour printer	Color LaserJet 4500 DN				
Hewlett Packard		2	2		
Speaker	Microsoft	7	7		
Digital camera	Digital DSC-F1	1	1		
Facsimile	Panasonic	1	1		
Fax-modem		1			
UPS		—			
Binding machine		1			
Refrigerator		1			
Copier	Canon	1			
Overhead projector		—			

Source: Telecentre Survey, December 2000

Table 4. Inventory of software

Software Manuals
Programmer manual
Internet training, management of an Internet server
Norton Manual
CD-ROM User's Manual
Digital Overhead Projector User's Manual
Complete Excel
CDS/ISIS Manual Version 2.3.

CD-ROMs
UNESCO Sahel Point
Library for Sustainable Development and Basic Needs
World Environment Library
Food and Nutrition Library
Medical and Health Library
Microsoft Windows 98
Access 2000
Easy Axess Video Conference Software,
Office Pro
Internet Training
Word and Excel Training

Services and patterns of use

The telecentre was offering a variety of ICT services including telephony, facsimile, Internet access, and email. The most popular services were scanning, telephone (both out-going and in-coming) and facsimile, text processing, printing, and photocopying. The services were used to get or send information on education, business or trade, and tourism. Telephone connection is provided by SOTELMA, the public telecommunications provider, the only one used by the Telecentre. Telecentre users pointed out that the telephone connection is unreliable.

There has been a definite rise in the number of users since the telecentre opened its doors in April 1999 (see Table 5). The table shows that women represented 23.2% of all users between April 1999 and February

2001. Telecentre records of registered users show that youth constituted 48.5%, adults 51.8%, and the elderly less than 2%. The majority of users (over 84%) went to the telecentre in the morning. The exit poll indicated that few women (10–29%) visited the telecentre during the period of observation. Information collected from other sources (e.g., community leaders, opinion leaders, associations, women groups, NGOs, and the telecentre management committee) corroborates the low patronage of women users.

The telephone and facsimile were very popular for communication, with 42% of visitors making calls and 37% receiving and 26% sending facsimiles. The most popular computer-related services were: word processing, training, and computer games. The telecentre was used most often for social reasons – to communicate with family and friends. The use of email and the Internet was quite low. Forty percent of the users visit to acquire computer skills; whereas, only 10% access the Internet from the telecentre.

Communication was frequently effected by letter or by phone rather than by email, and 31% of the respondents indicated that they send letters 'free of charge' because they were hand carried by a friend or relative. Eighteen percent of those surveyed had recently paid between FCFA 500 and 1,250 for phone calls to other towns (e.g., Bamako). Respondents try to reduce the cost of phone calls by using other alternatives. A little more than half of the people stated that they rarely made long distance calls; whereas, fewer than 10% paid between FCFA 2,000 and 3,000 for long distance calls.

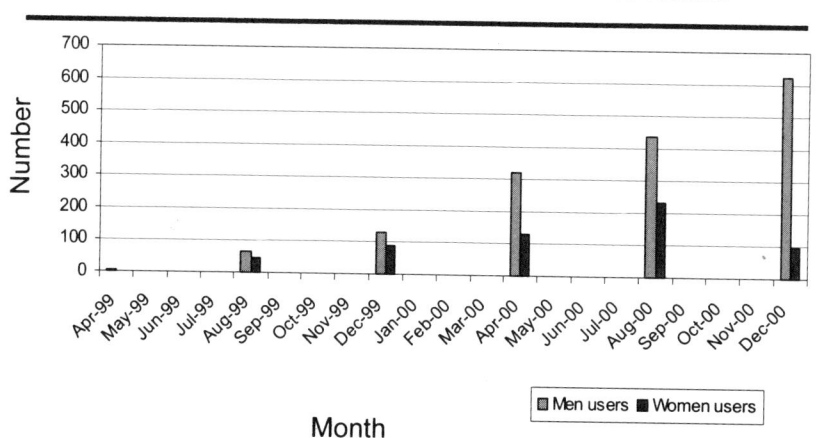

Figure 1. Timbuktu telecentre users for selected months

Table 5. Number of users in Timbuktu telecentre (April 1999–February 2001)

	Total Number of Users	Women Users (%)
April 1999	5	2 (40.0)
May 1999	97	32 (33.0)
June 1999	125	65 (52.0)
July 1999	84	29 (34.5)
August 1999	113	47 (41.6)
September 1999	69	29 (42.0)
October 1999	338	86 (25.4)
November 1999	454	91 (20.0)
December 1999	219	88 (40.2)
January 2000	331	73 (22.1)
February 2000	534	97 (18.2)
March 2000	499	179 (35.9)
April 2000	449	128 (28.5)
May 2000	384	98 (25.5)
June 2000	270	89 (33.0)
July 2000	557	87 (15.6)
August 2000	672	234 (34.8)
September 2000	650	202 (31.2)
October 2000	741	174 (23.5)
November 2000	921	140 (15.2)
December 2000	721	99 (13.7)
January 2001	891	119 (13.4)
February 2001	832	116 (13.9)
Total	9956	2304 (23.2)

The figures in Table 5 show a clearer picture of the difference between men and women users when presented graphically as seen in Figure 1. Also disadvantaged in terms of ICT access were the elderly. During 4 days of continuous observations, not a single person over 60 years of age visited the telecentre. Telecentre records also showed that of almost 4,000 users, only 11 (0.3%) were over 60 years of age. One participant in a focus group discussion had this say:

> Needless to say, young people can more easily adapt to ICTs and are more interested in using computer science, especially the Internet, to access educational information. Moreover, young 15-year-old school goers, including girls, are frequent TC users. In the evenings, they go to tinker on the computer once most of the regular customers have left. One of them spent 5 consecutive days studying for a geography lesson on 'Mali: A Physical Study.'

It was found that poor use or disadvantage was not a function of any serious physical barrier since access to the telecentre was within reasonable distance of the majority of actual or potential users. Most people (62%) who were interviewed lived less than 1 km from the telecentre. Another 31% lived between 1 and 3 km away. About three-quarters (74%) took less than 30 minutes to reach the telecentre, and all users reported that they often walked to the telecentre as they did to most other places (see Table 6).

User profiles

There are two types of users – individuals and legal entities or organizations. Among the individual users, 76.8 % were male and 23.2% were female. Youth represented 48% of all users. The users were generally educated, and the feeling that computers are for literate people was pervasive among respondents. A wide variety of professionals used the facility. Arabic speakers rarely visited the telecentre because there was no software in Arabic.

Legal entities or organizations that used the telecentre include cultural, scientific, educational, professional, tourist, development, and women's associations in addition to members of the police force and staff of independent radio stations. These various groups had between 50 and 1,000 members, whose ages ranged between 18 and 40 years. Community leaders constituted a separate and distinct group. Although organizational users

Table 6. Distance travelled, method of transport, and time taken to reach various sources of information in Timbuktu

Category	At home	Distance (km) 0–0.5	0.5–1	1–3	>3	Means Foot	Bike	Time (minutes) 0–10	11–30	31–60
Post office	—	19	21	20	5	65	—	31	27	7
Private telephone	9	28	19	9	3	65	—	47	16	2
Public telephone	12	28	12	13	0	65	—	43	19	3
Newspaper vendor	—	34	18	8	5	65	—	42	20	3
Bookshop	—	26	25	9	5	65	—	37	21	5
Cinema hall	—	—	—	—	—	—	—	—	—	—
Clinic/Hospital	—	19	29	15	2	65	—	33	27	5
Library	—	22	29	12	2	65	—	34	27	3
Telecentre	—	20	30	13	2	65	—	30	30	5

Source: Survey, December 2000.

were fewer than individual users, telecentre staff actively wooed them because of the volume of customers from them and also in order to establish a 'constituency of customers'.

In addition to the direct users, there were other secondary users or beneficiaries. They are all the men and women who enter into what some of the key informants referred to as 'contacts and dialogue networks' with the direct users. Through these networks, the direct users convey the information they have received from the telecentre. This circle is extensive and reaches out to friends, colleagues, and relatives among others.

Direct users conveyed and shared the information they received with third parties. Fourteen users who were interviewed when exiting the telecentre claimed to share information with 68 other people. These included fathers, mothers, brothers and sisters, spouses, aunts, uncles, and nephews. Fifty-seven percent of the users interviewed said they conveyed the information they obtain to others such as friends (41%), clients (26%), and colleagues (15%). Most of the non-user beneficiaries were between the ages of 31 and 50 years. Three categories of Timbuktu residents were considered to derive indirect benefits from the services of the telecentre:

- Members of the user's household and friends and colleagues with whom the user shares information;
- The non-user members of the associations and local agencies with whom the user shares information; and
- Business, social, and religious contacts.

In the December 2000 survey sample of 52 users and potential users, 47 were men and 5 were women. Forty-six percent of these users were between the ages of 31 and 40 years, 25% were between 21 and 30 years, and 21% were between 41 and 50 years. The exit poll indicated that of the 14 users interviewed, 4 were artisans, 2 were secretaries, 2 worked at radio stations, and 6 belonged to other professions. Among the artisans were a blacksmith, a cobbler, a tailor, and a driver. The 'other' professional category included a manager, an accountant, a computer hardware technician, a teacher, and an animal breeder.

Community leaders (e.g., Chair of the Chamber of Commerce, and President of the Youth Association) played a significant role in the Timbuktu telecentre both as a core group of users and as advisers to the project. There were differences in the types of services used by the different leaders.

For example, whereas the leaders of trade and commerce received training and used the Internet, the leader of the youth association used photocopying and document processing more heavily. It is particularly noteworthy that the leader of the women's organization, only used the facsimile and telephone.

Reasons for use/non use

The primary reasons for using the telecentre were to send, receive, process, or retrieve information (Table 7). Training was also important, as were activities related to preparing project applications of those organizations embarking on their own projects. Table 7 also shows the amount each organization paid for the services they received from the telecentre during the year 2000.

Table 7. Types of information, service used, and cost of using telecentres

Association Name	Information type sought	Service used	Cost per year (FCFA)
CAFO	Training Women's activities	Telephone/facsimile Letters Television Door to door	60 000
SAVAMA	Scientific, Cultural, Religious	Letters Telephone/facsimile Email Direct contacts	120 000
Chamber of Commerce	Artisanal	Internet Telephone/facsimile Email	180 000
GOUNA (Youth)	Political, Economic, Cultural	Telephone/facsimile Letters Radio	600 000
BOUCTOU	Tourist	Internet Email Telephone/facsimile	120 000

Source: Telecentre Survey, December 2000.

Associations and organizations were a significant source of revenue for the telecentre. The associations are organized in a network formed to support and facilitate the exchange of information among members as well as non-members. The associations and organizations usually communicate general information about their professions, culture, education, and tourism to each other and to third parties. The associations share information with national partners in Bamako, for example, and with international partners in Europe and in Arab, African, and Asian countries. The information communicated to external partners generally relates to development issues (especially fundraising for projects) and inquiries about potential trading partners. Information on culture and tourism is also popular.

Prominent among impediments to use and difficulties that impair the effective use of the MCT is connectivity. When the evaluation team arrived at the telecentre for the study, for example, the telephone connection had been interrupted. The telecentre staff also reported that delays in the procurement and installation of a VSAT for the telecentre had caused serious difficulties for project implementation. The other technical difficulties experienced by the telecentre are shown in Table 8.

Table 8. Common technical problems encountered at the telecentre

Type of problem	Solved by Staff	Solved by Someone else	Frequency of problem
Computer failure	X		Once in 4 months
Printer break down	X		Once in 3 months
Software not working	X		Every month
Routine computer servicing	X		Every month
Photocopier break down		X	Once in 6 months
Supplies out of stock	X		Once in 6 months
Internet network	X		Once in 6 months
Power interruption and failures		X	Every month
Telephone/connection Signal interruption		X	Every month
Busy tone		X	Every month

Source: Survey, December 2000.

The telecentre staff solved all computer and computer-related technical and printer breakdown problems. Of the ten problem types highlighted as common occurrences six were solved by the telecentre staff, a reflection of their technical competence and self-reliance. The telecentre also offered electronic equipment maintenance services to the public. However, the staff had no competence in dealing with photocopier problems electricity or telephone problems and had to rely on external assistance. The major hurdles encountered in dealing with technical problems were procurement of computer spares and getting the telecom provider (SOTELMA) to resolve problems related to the quality of service provided.

Other than the technical problems, another reason for low or non-use was the cost of services. Fifty percent of questionnaire respondents felt that high service charges, in relation to women's low purchasing power, were responsible for the small number of women using the ICTs. Close to two-thirds of the respondents (65%) expressed the belief that if prices were reduced there would be a significant increase in the number of women using the ICTs. A few steps had been taken by the Timbuktu telecentre to address the disadvantages that women suffer:

- Giving women visible positions of authority, e.g., as members of the telecentre management committee;
- Placing photos of women on the front pages of some documents showing them as trainers of men;
- Writing user manuals with women; and
- Providing a 25–50% discount on training fees for women.

Relevance and user satisfaction

Telecentre users were of the opinion that the services offered were relevant and useful because they:

- Opened up Timbuktu to the outside world;
- Enhance the speed and ease of external communications because the services were now available nearby;
- Provided rapid, sure, and affordable communication; and
- Promoted knowledge of computer technology.

They also believed that the best performing services were computer training, telephony, and facsimile transmission. The least developed of the services was content development

In September 2000 the MCT supported a study to identify and design appropriate content and applications for various organizations and projects. About one dozen projects were investigated, but the content or applications had not been developed at the time of the study due to an absence of expertise among the telecentre staff and the lack of funding. Apparently the development of applications and content is proving to be harder than first thought.

Perhaps on account of the troubles with content development and other technical difficulties user satisfaction with the MCT was a mixed bag. All users interviewed maintained that the services offered by the telecentre were relevant and useful. Responses identifying what they did not like were not so unanimous. The list included a number of different things. For example,

- Lack of connections (43%) – connectivity is perceived as a real issue;
- Small premises (36%) – the telecentre is in a temporary location that is too small to accommodate a large number of people at one time; and
- Insufficient machines – which cause users to interrupt training sessions and results in non-completion of practical training requirements.

Users also felt that their information needs with regard to email, Internet access, and advanced computer training were not being adequately met. They pointed out that there was a very long waiting list of people who had applied for training.

Associations and groups were also concerned about the quality and quantity of information they obtained, and some offered such judgements about the telecentre as: 'not good', 'has to be improved', and 'bad'. It was evident that the telecentre was not satisfying the needs of some of the users and they attributed their dissatisfaction to connection/connectivity difficulties at the centre.

Other users, however, declared that the telecentre had satisfied all their needs, and that they had succeeded in promoting their products and their profession at the international level. The telecentre was deemed to have failed in the following aspects: service organization and planning and financial management. Another sore point with the users was the delay in the construction of permanent premises. Unlike the unsatisfied users, the technical staff and the community leaders on the whole conveyed a favourable impression of the telecentre. They suggested that the telecentre was well managed and the telecentre and SOTELMA staff in Timbuktu highlighted some of its successful achievements to buttress their claims:

- Telecommunication staff: demystification of the computer, training of youth, and opening up of Timbuktu to the rest of the world;
- Key community leaders: support given to tourist guides and tourism; acquisition of new knowledge and opening to the world, improvements in communications quality and speed (authentic information in real time), proximity of ICTs, especially the Internet, and community training; and
- Staff, management, and management committee: promoting understanding and popularization of computer technology, time savings in business for traders, and tourist guides, creation of new services, and change in attitudes.

Sustainability

Management and ownership

Management has a direct impact on the sustainability of telecentres. With regard to ownership, project documents stipulate that the telecentre: '... shall be the property of the district of Timbuktu ... the latter may later decide to transfer the property rights ... to a consortium/cooperative of local partners or to a private entrepreneur'.

The management staff and committee indicated that they believed that ownership was not a simple issue and they could not state categorically or convincingly that the telecentre was, at the time of the inquiry, the property of the community. The staff expressed the view that: 'for the time being, no measures have been taken to solve this important issue, which is having an impact on the sustainability of the telecentre.' Users, on the other hand, were enthusiastic in their declaration that the telecentre belonged to the community of Timbuktu. As a matter of fact the management and property rights for daily management of the centre as seen in recruitment, supervision, provision of financial and material resources, and price setting were exercised by the management staff and the management committee on behalf of the community.

The local management committee, made up of leaders of government technical departments, the Town Hall, and community and telecentre representatives is supposed to be responsible for administrative and financial management (revenue control, control of daily expenses and procurements), and recruitment. However, a national coordinator (man), a staff member of SOTELMA, the national provider, and a manager were responsible for the daily supervision and financial management of the telecentre. The roles of the committee and the national coordinator were not very clearly delineated and this caused some problems. Membership of the management committee also created difficulties. Members are often civil servants who are regularly changed and this leads to an uncontrollable and continuous turnover of members, which in turn affects the smooth running of the telecentre. The management body was known under different names: management committee, local management committee, steering committee, and management and steering committee, which made it also confusing for the community. Committee members refered to it as the local management committee.

Community participation in management

Community leaders (e.g., the Chair of the CAFO, the Chair of the Chamber of Commerce, and the President of the Youth Association) played a significant role in the Timbuktu telecentre both as a core group of users and as advisers to the project. The community leaders acted as advisors in the setting up of the telecentre and actively participated in negotiations with the local authorities for the land on which the telecentre was constructed. Although all those interviewed stated that the telecentre belonged to the community, the nature of involvement of the community as owner in the daily management of the telecentre suggested a different interpretation. Table 9 suggests that the management committee was performing only a small fraction of its mandate and that the manager appeared to have usurped most of the committee functions. One community representative in the management committee confirmed his own participation in supervision and revenue control suggesting that perhaps the committee was working as intended. But this was questionable; the exact nature of this supervision was neither clear nor apparently highly valued since the telecentre staff were also subject to supervision by officers located in the project executing agency, SOTELMA, the government telecom.

The wider community involvement in fund-raising was clear and appreciated. Funds were being raised for the telecentre building that was under construction. Fund-raising activities included community members organizing artistic and cultural events, making contributions of FCFA100 per family, and making personal and group contributions and grants.

Table 9. Community involvement in telecentre management

Involvement	Manager	Management Committee
Staff recruitment	X	
Supervision	X	X
Provision of financial and material resources	X	
Price fixation	X	
Administration	X	
Financial management	X	
Revenue control	X	X
Control of daily expenses and procurements	X	

Source: Telecentre Survey, December 2000.

Although they were very involved with fund-raising, community members were not involved in the planning, running, and maintenance of the centre. The management staff were in full control of all these tasks. It was reported that, this has been a source of some disaffection for community members. They complained that they did not receive regular reports and feedback and pointed to this as being a sign of inefficiency. Community participation in management has been restricted to revenue control, possibly in compliance with funders' requirements for community participation. Nevertheless, it was recognized that participation through representation of various social and socio-professional community groups in the management committee is important for the sustainability of the telecentres.

Telecentre finances

The telecentre depends primarily on donor funds to support its activities. Total partners' grants to the telecentre amounted to just over FCFA 213 million in February 2001. This money was used initially to fund a launching seminar for the telecentre, recruit the coordinator, and purchase equipment. The staff was still being paid from project funds, and the telecentre was still a project of the three original principal partners, UNESCO, ITU, and IDRC. Supplementary funds were also being received from other donors. Revenues for services provided by the telecentre between 1999 and 2001 are shown in Table 10.

Although there have been significant increases in revenue between May 1999 and February 2001, it is impossible to determine the financial viability of the telecentre based on the available information because there was neither a general income statement nor a balance sheet at the time of the investigation. Although financial sustainability could not be adequately determined, the research did suggest several other factors that may contribute to the potential sustainability of the telecentre in Timbuktu:

- A conducive political and sociocultural context. For example, 'the political parties and civil society have committed themselves to the success of the telecentre';
- The economic necessities and resources exist to support the telecentre. The town's major activities are trade, agriculture (market gardening), handicraft, tourism and hospitality services. Timbuktu is an important economic centre, a crossroads for several traders, and a melting pot for a number of cultures (e.g., Berber, Islam, Modern, African, and French);
- Timbuktu has historical significance and is a tourist centre of world renown;
- Timbuktu is technically equipped to support the services.

The researchers involved in the study believe that the context of the ancient town remains generally favourable for the development and sustainability of the Timbuktu telecentre. It is averred that all the significant political and development actors including the political parties, local administration, traditional associations, and NGOs, have great expectations for the telecentre. Faith it seems requires to be backed with some reasonableness

Table 10. Telecentre revenue (1999 to 2001)

Month	Telecentre revenue (FCFA)
May 1999	19 500
June 1999	32 850
July 1999	31 250
August 1999	11 650
September 1999	71 500
October 1999	55 100
November 1999	36 800
December 1999	80 850
Total 1999	**339 500**
January 2000	222 330
February 2000	142 845
March 2000	184 540
April 2000	107 510
May 2000	254 475
June 2000	372 875
July 2000	267 850
August 2000	426 680
September 2000	189 870
October 2000	418 250
November 2000	483 120
December 2000	300 740
Total 2000	**3 371 085**
January 2001	315 957
February 2001	595 675
Total 2001	**911 632**
Grand total	**4 622 217**

Source: Survey; telecentre records.

and the staff and management committee members were aware of the need for sustainability and enumerated several factors that were affecting the MCTs income-generating capacity:

- The premises were too small for a telecentre, which meant that the large number of customers was cramped in the available space and privacy could not be guaranteed;
- Connectivity problems were persistent and, as a result, it was nearly impossible to have one week of continuous unbroken telephone connection, which greatly discouraged customers and needless to say grievously damaged incomes;
- Local capacity building is required to improve service delivery in the following skill areas: Internet, virtual communities, and educational strategies. Telecentre staff need training in project management, marketing, organization and support of virtual communities, equipment repairs and maintenance, technical repairs, education, office automation, the elaboration and application of accounting management tools including budget planning, income and expenditure accounting and the preparation of balance sheets.

The above impediments notwithstanding, it must not be forgotten that the initial intention and motivation was not to create a super successful capitalist venture but a flagship pilot project which would demonstrate some of the potentials and challenges of pursuing and providing public access in the difficult technical terrain of developing countries. Nowhere in the project objectives is it stated that the project would be making x amount of profit by so or so year. On the contrary, the project was to test the idea and the technologies for public access. Of course, in time, issues of sustainability would arise, by which time the tools and methods for both assuring sustainability and for measuring this dimension would have been worked into project designs from the start. It therefore seems that what ought to be measured at this historical period ought to be the validity of the concept of telecentres and the reliability of the technologies and management models for the kinds of environments into which they have been introduced.

Summary and conclusion

Although evidence of financial sustainability is lacking, the signs and impressions gathered suggest some positive effects that can be attributed to the pilot project in Timbuktu. Some changes observed seemed to have been related, to some extent, to the telecentre:

- The telecentre has created ICT services in the vicinity of Timbuktu. The opening of Timbuktu through communication has had a positive effect on business and tourism. Communication has been made easy, it is fast and affordable, and it takes place in real time;
- The telecentre has contributed to the pool of modern telecommunications equipment and services in the town;
- The telecentre has provided computer training for community members and this exposure to new ICTs has brought about a change in attitudes and knowledge;
- Other knowledge-related capacities have been developed among community members (e.g., librarians have been trained to use UNESCO's computerized library automation software).

Experiences from the multipurpose community telecentre project in Timbuktu show that there are major lessons still to be learned and that a wide range of capacities must be developed to support a telecentre. However, the importance of the efforts to popularize the telecentre and the political support that was received should not be undervalued. People's lives, attitudes, knowledge, and perceptions are changing. The young blacksmith who now regularly sends emails to his contacts abroad is ample evidence that the computer has become a familiar tool in daily life. This situation is not about to change. The challenge is now to build upon the experiences of the telecentre in Timbuktu so that new projects can address the weaknesses that were demonstrated in this pilot project.

Chapter 4

Telecentres in Mozambique

Occupying 801,590 km^2 in southeastern Africa, Mozambique, which won independence from Portugal in 1975, is ranked among the world's poorest countries with a GNP per capita of USD 230 in 1999 (World Bank 2000). Approximately 78.3% of its over 17 million people spend less than USD 2 per day. The quality of life for the majority of Mozambicans is poor: under-five mortality is 213 per 1,000; life expectancy at birth is 45.5 years; and adult illiteracy is 58% among Mozambicans over 15 years of age. The electric power consumption per capita was 47 kilowatt-hours in 1997, and in 1998 only 18.7% of the roads in the entire country were paved.

The current situation in Mozambique can be traced partly to the long and destructive civil war that ravaged the country for more than a decade ending in 1992. The problems have also been exacerbated by its proximity to Zimbabwe and South Africa, which were systems of apartheid. More recently in 2000, floods and cyclones devastated the southern and central parts of the country and wiped out many of the gains made since the end of the civil war in the early 1990s.

Telecommunications context

Mozambique is one of 25 countries in Africa that have established an independent telecommunications regulatory authority, and by the end of 2000 it had an Informatics Policy and National Information and Communication Infrastructure (NICI) plan in place to spur growth in the underdeveloped sector. It is expected that the policy and plan will enable the state to subsidize telecommunications services and reduce the cost of computer equipment.

There is one fixed line operator (Telecomunicaçies de Mocambique) and one mobile operator. The fixed line tele-density was 0.51 in 2001while the mobile tele-density was 0.80. Cellular phone services were launched in Mozambique in 1997 and by 2001, there were approximately 140,000 subscribers. There were 1,251 telephones in 2000 and 11,948 Internet subscribers.

Access to other forms of ICTs such as newspapers, radios, and televisions is generally poor in Mozambique. Available figures indicate that only 3 in every 1,000 people had access to daily newspapers in 1996; 40 in 1,000 had radios in 1997; and 5 in 1,000 had access to televisions.

Two telecentres, located in Manhiça and Namaacha, were the focus of this study, which was conducted over 2 weeks in August 2000. Two types of questionnaires were used to collect information from 238 users and 976 potential users (including staff and students). Interviews and group discussions were also held with telecentre staff, members of the local management committees, and representatives of other institutions in Manhiça and Namaacha.

Telecentre context

Telecentres as institutions providing access to various types of ICTs were first introduced to Mozambique through the Eduardo Mondlane University Informatics Centre (CIUEM). In 1999, CIUEM implemented a pilot project with support from the International Development Research Centre (IDRC) in which two telecentres were set up in the districts of Manhiça and Namaacha.

The districts of Manhiça and Namaacha share certain similarities. Similar in size, both lie within Maputo province and are easily accessible from Maputo, the capital city of Mozambique, which is about 74 km away on good highways. Inhabitants of both districts speak Shangana and Ronga (the local languages) and Portuguese, the official language of the country. Most government ministries are present in both districts as district directorates: the Directorates of Education, Health, Agriculture, Culture, Youth and Sport, Industry and Trade, and Public Works and Housing.

Manhiça District, located in northern Maputo Province, has a population of 130,000 and is characterized by high rates of migration by men to South African mines for employment. Manhiça has some industrial potential in the areas of Maragara, Xinavane, and Palmeira. It has 39 institutions and enterprises, which include nine state institutions, five political parties, four agro-industrial companies, two financial institutions, one agency of the Mozambique Telecommunications Company (TDM), one agency of the Mozambique Electricity Company (EDM), seven commercial establishments and hotels, and ten non-governmental organizations (NGOs). Manhiça also has one secondary school, one middle-level teacher-training institute, and a number of primary schools.

Namaacha District borders Swaziland and is located in southern Maputo province. With an estimated population of 31,259, Namaacha is an area with tourism potential. The inhabitants of the district are generally petty traders. There are twenty-eight institutions and enterprises in the district, which include nine state institutions, five political parties, two financial institutions, one agro-industrial company, one agency for TDM and EDM, five commercial establishments and hotels, and five NGOs. Namaacha also has one secondary school, one basic-level teacher training centre, and a number of primary schools.

Telecentre locations

Both the Manhiça and Namaacha telecentres are easy to reach because they are both located in the centre of their respective districts. The Manhiça telecentre occupies 75 m^2 in a building owned by the Castro Restaurant, while the Namaacha telecentre occupies 120 m^2 in the Namaacha Secondary School. There is little similarity in the physical layout of the two telecentres. Manhiça, like Nakaseke in Uganda, is one continuous room with no divisions between the various areas of the centre. Namaacha is organized to allow for clearly designated spaces for the different services that are offered, one of the few with such a plan.

Profile of users

The majority of users come to the telecentres in a personal capacity (81.1%) as opposed to representing institutions (18.9%). On the whole, males tended to dominate the use of the two telecentres. Of a total of 222 respondents, only 35.6% were female. The gender gap was wider in Manhiça, where men and boys constituted about three-quarters of the users. The gender differences in Namaacha were relatively narrower (see Table 12).

Although users of all ages could be found in the telecentres, users were overwhelmingly below the age of 40 (Table 13). The most active age group was between 17 and 25 years of age. In fact, at Namaacha, the 17–25-year user group constituted over 50% of all visitors to the telecentre.

In addition, the survey found that about 50% of the respondents had a secondary school education, and that 63% of the users were students. These findings confirm that most telecentre users were young. It is not surprising that approximately 75% of the users in Namaacha were secondary school students given that the telecentre is located within the grounds of a secondary school. Adult users included teachers from other schools in the town and a small number of other people with educational backgrounds ranging from those who were illiterate to those with a fourth grade education.

Although the users at Manhiça were also young, they came from different sectors of activity, not just schools. This is perhaps due to the fact that the telecentre is located by a national highway, in an area that is reasonably 'independent' of any institution, i.e., did not give the impression that it was mainly for the use of members of that institution. Namaacha telecentre in comparison appeared to give the impression that the telecentre was for the exclusive use of the school.

Table 11. Sex of telecentre users in Manhiça and Namaacha

Telecentre	Female	Male	Total number
Manhiça	24 (25.8%)	69 (74.2%)	93
Namaacha	55 (42.6%)	74 (57.4%)	129
Total	79	143	222

Source: Survey, August 2000.

Table 12. Age of telecentre users in Manhiça and Namaacha

Telecentre	0–16 years	17–25 years	26–40 years	Over 40 years	Total
Manhiça	15 (16.7%)	39 (43.3%)	30 (33.3%)	6 (6.7%)	90
Namaacha	31 (23.8%)	74 (56.9%)	21 (16.2%)	4 (3.1%)	130
Total	46	113	51	10	220

Source: Survey, August 2000.

An overwhelming majority of the users were urban dwellers who lived in the district capitals of Manhiça (76.1%) and Namaacha (94.8%). During data collection, a period which extended over 2 weeks, only one person visited the telecentre from a different district (Moamba), some 20 km away. This suggests that visitors from other districts used the telecentres. Conversations with telecentre staff and partners at Manhiça confirmed that users also came from the districts of Magude and Xinavane.

Equipment and services offered

A variety of equipment and material was available at the two telecentres: computers, photocopiers, facsimile machines, telephones, television sets, video cassette recorders, and print materials. Among the services offered were Internet access, email, word processing, photocopying, scanning, faxing, telephony, television and video viewing, library services, and training.

Frequency of use

In Manhiça, the same users went to the telecentre daily, some more than three times each day. The users came from the town and some neighbouring villages and districts, some as far away as 10–30 km. Table 14 shows the frequency of use of each service by males and females. Users were asked how often they used the services in pre-defined periods of 1 day, 1 week, and 1 month. The users had to specify whether they used a given service 5 days per week (5 D/W), 3–4 days per week (3–4 D/W), 1–2 days per week (1–2 D/W), 2 days per month (2 D/M), or 1 day per month (1 D/M). The figures in the table suggest that as the frequency of use increased, the number of women users decreased. Fifty-four percent men and 46% women used the centres one day each month, while 71% men and 29% women used them five times each week.

Generally, use was lower among females. Twice as many women used the Namaacha Telecentre (39%) as Manhiça (18%). The corresponding percentage of men users was 82% for Manhiça and 61% in Namaacha. In both telecentres, the most commonly used services were photocopying, computers for word processing and telephones, and the least used services were email, facsimile, and Internet access. Data for differential service use shows the telephone to have been most popular with the women whereas with the men it was photocopying and computer word processing.

Figure 2. Service used by sex in Manhiça and Namaacha

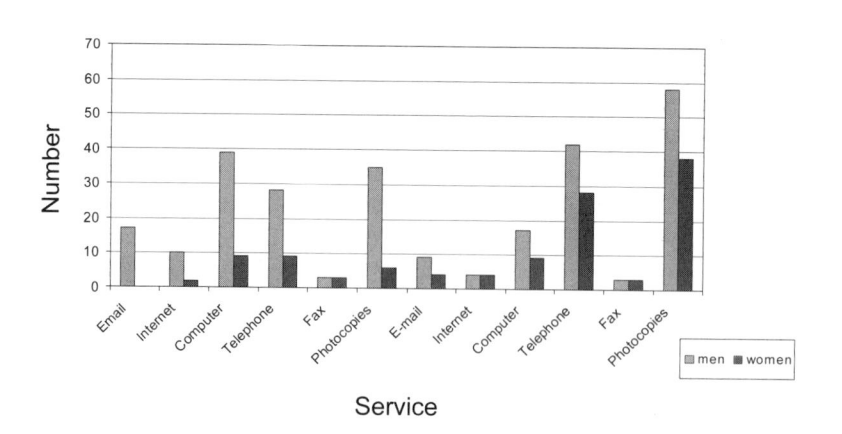

Table 13. Frequency of use of telecentre services by men (M) and women (F)

		5 D/W M	5 D/W F	3-4D/W M	3-4D/W F	1-2D/W M	1-2D/W F	2D/M M	2D/M F	1D/M M	1D/M F	Total (%) M	Total (%) F
Manhiça	Email	4	0	0	0	9	0	2	0	2	0	17	0
	Internet	4	0	0	0	3	1	3	0	0	1	10	2
	Computer	13	7	11	2	8	0	3	0	4	0	39	9
	Telephone	6	3	9	2	10	2	2	1	1	1	28	9
	Fax	1	0	1	1	0	1	1	1	0	0	3	3
	Photocopies	6	1	11	0	6	1	5	2	7	2	35	6
Total												132 (82)	29 (18)
Namaacha	E-mail	3	1	2	0	2	2	1	0	1	1	9	4
	Internet	1	0	0	2	1	1	1	0	1	1	4	4
	Computer	9	2	1	2	5	5	1	0	1	0	17	9
	Telephone	12	10	16	8	11	9	3	0	0	1	42	28
	Fax	2	1	0	0	1	2	0	0	0	0	3	3
	Photocopies	12	4	3	6	27	4	4	5	2	9	58	38
Total												133 (61)	86 (39)
Total		72	29	54	23	83	28	26	9	19	16	265	115
Total %		71	29	70	30	75	25	74	26	54	46	70	30

Source: User Survey, August 2000.

Table 14. Service used by sex in Manhiça and Namaacha

		M	(%)	F	(%)
Manhiça	Email	17	(100)	0	(0)
	Internet	10	(83)	2	(17)
	Computer	39	(81)	9	(19)
	Telephone	28	(76)	9	(24)
	Fax	3	(50)	3	(50)
	Photocopies	35	(85)	6	(15)
Namaacha	E-mail	9	(69)	4	(31)
	Internet	4	(50)	4	(50)
	Computer	17	(65)	9	(35)
	Telephone	42	(60)	28	(40)
	Fax	3	(50)	3	(50)
	Photocopies	58	(60)	38	(40)

Source: Culled from Table 13.

A rank ordering of the most popular services based on the figures in tables 13 and 14 show that for women the order was telephone, photocopying and computer word processing in a descending order of use. For men, the reverse order was observed with computers as the most used and telephones the least used of the popular services.

Purpose of use

Telecentre services (email, facsimile, and telephone) were used for exchanging messages with relatives, friends, commercial partners, and counterpart institutions. The computers were used for several purposes, including word and data processing and entertainment (e.g., games). Most users required photocopying services for reproducing personal documents, school materials, and various documents for local institutions and administrative and economic agencies. At the time of the study, only the Commercial Bank of Mozambique had a photocopier in the entire area.

Most email users could manipulate the systems and software by themselves, but a few required the help of others because they were unfamiliar with email technology, lacked knowledge about how to use the computers, or were illiterate.

Impediments to use

In addition to problems related to illiteracy and unfamiliarity with the new technologies, several other impediments to the use of the telecentres were identified:

- Lack of publicity: Some people indicated that they did not use the telecentres because they were unaware of their existence; there was a lack of publicity in the communities about the facilities provided by the telecentres;
- Relatively high cost of use: Not all the users could afford to pay the fees being charged for some of the services, e.g., computer training courses, because of the low levels of household income of the residents of Manhiça and Namaacha districts. The Internet service was hardly used because of the related telephone costs;
- Poor physical facilities: The toilets in the telecentres were in extremely poor condition, were old, and not very clean; the Manhiça telecentre operates out of very small, cramped premises making the experience uncomfortable; the Manhiça telecentre operates alongside a church with daily services; there were only three computers for the users and one for the staff; and the library collection was not sufficiently diversified; and
- Poor infrastructure: Frequent interruptions of electrical supply were a major source of disruption at the Namaacha Telecentre, and in the district in general.

Relevance

The services provided to the Manhiça and Namaacha communities were reported to be of acceptable quality, despite the problems of constant power cuts at Namaacha, which affected the quality of some services. The quality of the Internet services was less than adequate because of the sluggish dial-up connection. The other services met the users' needs and expectations. The users considered the telecentres to be extremely important for their daily activities. The only public photocopying services in the two districts were to be found in the telecentres. Alternative photocopiers, in a bank in Manhiça and a hotel in Namaacha, were charging five times the price charged in the telecentres. This was also true of the telephones – the only other public telephone was to be found at the telephone exchange.

Users were also asked to indicate what type of information they would like to have available and to rate how important this information was to them. The 933 respondents would like, in order of importance, information about: education, health care, sports, government information, trade, agriculture, religion, culture, weather, and entertainment. The three most important types of information identified by potential users were education, health, while sports, and culture, weather, and entertainment were considered to be less important.

User satisfaction

Interviewees expressed satisfaction with the fact that the telecentres were accessible to community members, who could now make use of ICTs and had the opportunity to communicate with the rest of the world. They also expressed satisfaction with what they described as effective use of photocopying, telephone, facsimile, and computer services at relatively low prices. The good qualities and qualifications of the telecentre staff were also appreciated.

Organizational users pointed out the benefits to their organizations of the use of the telecentres:

- Training workers in the use of computers;
- Typing, photocopying, and binding products at relatively low prices;
- Reducing postal costs due to the use of email;
- Reducing the use of human messengers for communication;
- Accessing information about goods and services both regionally and globally; and
- Facilitating the exchange of information between commercial partners.

Management, ownership, and sustainability

CIUEM has remained the implementing agency for the pilot project since it was started in 1999. It is regarded as the local owner of the initiative (Macome and Cumbana 2001). CIUEM has provided technical, financial, and management support to the telecentres.

Two male staff members in each telecentre were responsible for the day-to-day management of the telecentres. They had received technical and financial management training and could therefore handle low-level maintenance of computer equipment. A Local Advisory Committee (CAL) was formed for each of the telecentres as a way to involve local community members in the management of the telecentres. The CALs were charged with responsibility for the supervision and monitoring of telecentre activities. It was noted during the study that the Namaacha CAL had not made much contribution to the success of the telecentre because it was not very dynamic and lacked focus. When the investigations were conducted, CIUEM was preparing to hand over the management of the telecentres to the CALs, which were, along with the staff, being prepared to fully adopt the telecentres as community projects.

For the Manhiça and Namaacha telecentres, the factors that were considered to be essential for long-term sustainability were: the telecentres must own their own space; each telecentre should have a detailed financial analysis (which was not done in the present study); effective management teams must be identified and installed to ensure continuity; and government subsidies are necessary to reduce the cost of telephone services and computer equipment.

Conclusion and recommendations

The establishment of the Manhiça and Namaacha telecentres has made positive contributions. The telecentres were directly responsible for computer training, email, Internet, and library services being introduced into the districts. The telecentre users expressed great satisfaction with the telecentres because they were now able to use facilities that had previously only been available in the major cities of the country. The telecentres also had a positive impact on the organizations in the districts of Manhiça and Namaacha, and in the community in general, because they reduced the need for travel to Maputo to search of services or to communicate with relatives, business partners, and others. On the basis of the findings, it is recommended that:

- To ensure effective email and Internet services, a dedicated phone line to link the telecentres to the CIUEM, or an Internet and email server, should be installed in the telecentres;
- The telecentres should acquire premises of their own because, after the pilot phase, the telecentres may not be able to sustain themselves because of having to pay rent in addition to wages and other operational costs;
- Prices should be revised, especially for such services as word processing and the production of cards and invitations, and a system of subsidies should be introduced for students and low-income earners;
- Hours of operation should be revised to allow users to have access to the telecentres outside of normal working hours. The telecentres should remain open for longer hours and organize outreach activities focussed on the outlying regions of the district; and
- The telecentre should publish a local newspaper or bulletin, introduce other courses (e.g., accountancy, English language, keyboarding), install scanners, sell school materials and books, and acquire a colour photocopier.

Chapter 5

Telecentres in Uganda

Uganda is a multi-racial, multi-ethnic, and multi-religious landlocked country of 241,038 km^2 with an estimated population of about 20 million. The population density based on the 1991 census was 85 people/km^2, much higher than that of its neighbours in eastern Africa (31 people/km^2). Only 13.4% of the total population lives in urban centres; however, the rate of urbanization is increasing mainly because of migration during and after the civil wars. The size of the urban population is projected to increase to 8,876,000 by 2016 – an increase of 370% from 1991.

In 1992, Uganda, among the world's poorest countries, had a per capita income of under USD 170 (World Bank 1993). Uganda's economy is predominantly agricultural, with over 80% of the population depending directly or indirectly on the land. In 1998–99, agriculture contributed about 43% to overall GDP, with food crops accounting for over 28% of the agricultural output. However, the contribution from the agricultural sector to the overall GDP has declined due to structural changes in economic activity over the past dozen years. This trend reflects a reduction in the reliance of the economy on agriculture.

There has been a remarkable improvement in overall GDP. In 1998–99, real GDP achieved a growth rate of 7.8% in comparison with growth rates of 5.4% in 1997–98 and 4.5% in 1996–97. Per capita GDP grew from 1.7% in 1996–97 to 5.1% in 1998–99, and per capita income now stands at USD300. Despite Uganda's impressive growth rate, poverty is pervasive and income inequality persistent.

A republic since independence in 1962, Uganda has a decentralized administrative structure. District Local Councils (DLCs), headed by chairpersons, are at the apex of the local administration, which has five tiers of local government linked to the central government. The five tiers are usually referred to as: district level (LC5); county level (LC4); sub-county level (LC3); parish level (LC2); and village or village groups (LC1).

Telecommunications context

Uganda is often cited as a model case for good telecommunications development practice. In the early 1990s, the country was described as being 'seriously underdeveloped' in terms of telecommunications and services were much worse than the regional average. The situation significantly changed after reforms, which started in 1994, and dramatically changed the telecommunications environment placing Uganda ahead of its East African neighbours in matters of institutional and service innovations, e.g., the deployment of ISDN, falling tariffs and an appreciable increase in teledensity. Unlike its northern neighbour, VSAT and other service licenses have been issued with relative ease and interconnectivity resolved. Interconnectivity is a major headache for many national telecommunications providers where one or more mobile service providers exist alongside the incumbent or primary national operator. A 2000–2001 review of telecommunications objectives pledged that counties with populations of 500,000 and over would have basic access to telephony and an Internet POP would be established in every district to enhance the use of telecentres and similar services. The Uganda Communications Commission (UCC) is the chief proponent of these positive changes.

The UCC was set up by the government to improve communication services and bring operations in line with global developments and expectations. The Uganda Communications Act of 1997 mandated the Commission to:

- Ensure fair-play among service providers;
- Provide general protection to customers;
- Eliminate political interference in the communications sector; and
- Enhance national coverage of communication services.

In pursuance of the last objective, the Act provided for the establishment of a Rural Communications Development Fund (RCDF) as the means to achieve the objective of universal access. The RCDF has been established, and the fund is being used to leverage investments in rural communications services from the private sector (service providers and investors) and non-governmental organizations (NGOs) on a competitive basis. In 2002, the fund obtained a USD5-million grant from the World Bank to support the establishment of public phone centres, access points and Internet POPs in rural districts. A national ICT policy framework (UNCST 2001) and a rural communications development policy (UCC 2001) have been drafted, but are yet to be approved by parliament and made into law.

Uganda liberalized its communications sector early with the introduction of Celtel a mobile operator, which was joined by Mobile Telephone Network (MTN) in 1998. The Uganda Telecom Limited (UTL) and Uganda Posts Limited (UPL) were created from the former Uganda Posts and Telecommunications Corporation (UPTC) in 1997 and UTL remains the main provider of telephone landlines in the country (see Table 16). MTN was granted an operating license for both fixed and mobile service but unlike the mobile service, which has spread to major towns across the country, the fixed line service has been mostly used for corporate and business clients in and around Kampala. A major reason for this is the state of infrastructure. UTL and MTN have deployed fibre optic rings around Kampala in a metropolitan area network (MAN) that also uses the existing copper access network (Hamilton 2002). At the time of the study, there were three mobile telephone operators in Uganda (MTN, UTL, and Celtel), and in the last 2 years the telephone density has tripled on account of the increase in mobile telephony.

At the end of 1997, UTL had an installed capacity of 79,825 lines and 50,829 subscribers, accounting for a telephone density of 0.28 lines per 100 people. Seventy-three percent of all the lines in service are in Kampala. In rural areas, users have to travel, on average, 24 km to reach the nearest telephone (Uganda Bureau of Statistics 2001).

Uganda has a fledgling Internet market served by more than ten licensed Internet Service Providers (ISPs) with a current subscriber base of about 6,000, which is growing by 50–100% each year. Almost all of the subscribers are located in Kampala. Uganda, like Mozambique and unlike Mali and Senegal, does not have a policy of local dial-up tariff for Internet access.

Table 15. Telecommunications indicators, December 1996 to July 2001

Service provided	Dec 1996	Oct 1998	Dec 1999	Feb 2001	July 2001
Wired telephone lines (UTL)	45,145	55,749	57,913	58,880	52,054
Fixed wireless lines (MTN)	Not operational	148	447	932	1,900
Fixed wireless pay phones (MTN)	Not operational	0	200	1,650	2,195
Mobile cellular subscribers	3,000	12,000	72,602	188,568	276,034
-Celtel	3,000	8,100	19,074	32,934	40,000
-MTN	—	3,900	53,528	146,634	185,734
-UTL	—	—	—	10,000	50,300
Internet/email subscribers	504	1,308	4,248	5,688	5,999
National telecommunications operators	1	2	2	2	2
Mobile cellular operators (Celtel, MTN, UTL)	1	2	2	3	3
VSAT international data gateways (include UTL & MTN)	2	3	7	8	8
Internet service providers	2	7	9	11	11
Public pay communications network services	1	10	30	42	47
Private FM radio stations	14	28	37	100	112
Private television stations	4	8	11	19	20
Private radio communication licenses	453	530	688	770	800
National postal operator	1	1	1	1	1
Courier service providers	2	7	11	10	10

Source: UCC 2001.

Telecentre context

Three telecentres (MCTs) and two cybercafés were the subject of the investigations reported in this chapter. The three multipurpose community telecentres (MCTs) in the study were those in Nakaseke (reputed to be the first such facility in Africa), Nabweru, and Buwama. The cybercafés were in Bugolobi and Wandegeya, both located in Kampala. Data was collected from 889 individuals in January 2001 using a variety of instruments, which included a questionnaire and, interview, observation, discussion, and document-analysis guides in addition to an exit poll.

Wandegeya Cyber-Mart

The Wandegeya Cyber-Mart is located in one of the city's suburbs (Wandegeya), about 2 km north of Kampala city centre. Wandegeya is a small trading centre with a few shops, food kiosks, and a fairly big food market. Most of Wandegeya's shoppers reside in the nearby slums of Katanga and Makerere-Kivulu. To the east of the trading centre is the Wandegeya National Housing Estate, which is home to mostly middle-income civil servants and Makerere University. Makerere University is among East Africa's biggest universities with a student population of over 20,000. The cybercafé is situated a few hundred metres from both the housing estate and the university.

Bugolobi Business Centre

The Bugolobi Business Centre is located in the centre of the Bugolobi trading centre, about 3 km from Kampala city centre. The trading centre is quite small, with a handful of shops and a sizeable fruit and vegetable market. Bugolobi is situated near a large residential housing estate, the Bugolobi National Housing Estate, which is inhabited by both the well-off and the poor.

Buwama Telecentre

The Buwama telecentre is located in Buwama sub-county in Mpigi District. The sub-county covers about 39 km^2, and its headquarters, Buwama, is approximately 64 km from Kampala in southwestern Uganda. The sub-county consists of 10 administrative parishes and 57 villages. The one major trading centre in the sub-county is in Buwama, where the telecentre became operational in June 1999. The sub-county has a population of 350,000 and a 30% literacy rate (according to the census of 1991) and about 6,824 households.

Coffee farming, horticulture, and fishing in Lake Victoria are the main economic activities. Subsistence farming of bananas, sweet potatoes, and cassava is hugely popular, and the sub-county is generally food secure all year round. There are only two health centres and one sub-dispensary in the sub-county.

The information and communication network in the sub-county is very poor with only one sub-post office. Telephone services (cellular network) have been introduced recently after more than 15 years of non-existence. The Buwama telecentre is one of two, the other being Nabweru, started as part of the Acacia Initiative.

Nabweru Telecentre

The Nabweru telecentre is located at Nabweru sub-county headquarters in Mpigi District, approximately 6 km northwest of Kampala. It is in a periurban sub-county bordering Kampala that is made up of 6 parishes, 26 villages, and 3 major trading centres located at Nansana, Kawanda, and Kawempe. The telecentre situated in Kazo-Nabweru parish was opened in May 1999.

The sub-county covers about 25 km^2 and has about 53,290 inhabitants. Nabweru is one of the fastest growing sub-counties in the district. The major economic activities are trading and farming, and the sub-county is dotted with small trading centres and small-scale agro-processing industries for maize and coffee. There are 1,103 businesses (mostly retail shops), 8,000 farming families, 4 health centres, 27 clinics, and 21 drug shops in the sub-county.

Nakaseke Telecentre

The Nakaseke telecentre is located in Nakaseke sub-county in Luwero District about 44 km north of Kampala. The Nakaseke telecentre was opened in March 1999 as the first rural telecentre in Uganda. It was a project of a number of national and international donors: IDRC Acacia, the International Telecommunications Union (ITU), and UNESCO, among others.

Nakaseke sub-county is divided into five administrative parishes, which consist of 42 villages and an estimated population of 18,000 in 1998. The sub-county had one hospital and a relatively good educational infrastructure, which included 23 primary schools, 4 private secondary schools, and a primary teacher training college. The dominant economic activities in Nakaseke are crop and animal farming.

When the telecentre became operational in 1999, there was only one fixed telephone line in Nakaseke. By the time of the study about 2 years later, the telecommunications infrastructure had expanded to 250 lines and there were two public phones in the sub-county in addition to the two in the telecentre. Mobile telephony had also reached the sub-county with 15 individuals owning mobile phones.

Figure 3. Location of community telecentres, Uganda

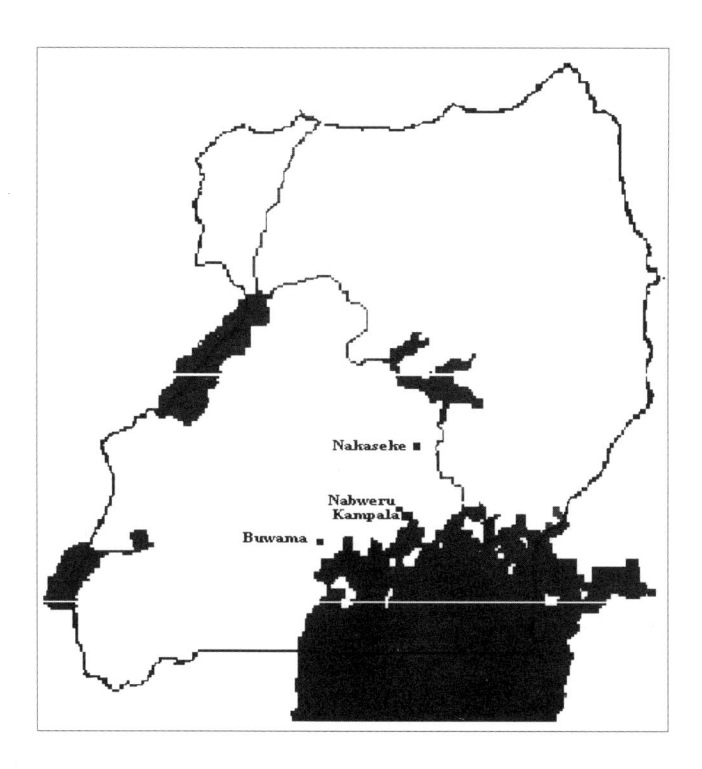

Findings

Facilities

All three multipurpose community telecentres were being housed free of charge either in public community centres (Buwama and Nakaseke) or in government buildings (Nabweru). The two cybercafés (Wandegeya and Bugolobi) were operating from rented premises.

In all but one of the facilities, Wandegeya Cyber-Mart, staff indicated that they did not have sufficient workspace, especially for administrative purposes. Only in Nabweru and Nakaseke were there separate offices for the managers. Furniture was adequate in both Buwama and the private cybercafés, but Nabweru and Nakaseke indicated that chairs were in short supply (Table 16). Nakaseke had five times as many chairs as the other multipurpose community telecentres, but the staff still considered this number insufficient. This was on account of the library, which attracted many users who, unlike users of other services, tended to stay longer. Table 16 shows the space occupied by each of the telecentres and the opinions of staff with respect to its adequacy. Surprisingly, only in the smallest telecentre was space considered adequate.

Table 16. Facilities at community telecentres and private cybercafés

	Rooms occupied	Estimated space (m^2)	Space adequate?	Number of chairs	Chairs adequate?
Buwama	2	88	No	10	Yes
Nabweru	3	72	No	10	No
Nakaseke	3	178	No	50	No
Wandegeya	1	60	Yes	22	Yes
Bugolobi	3	82	No	6	Yes

Source: Survey 2001.

Table 17. Equipment available and in actual use in the telecentres and cybercafés*

	Buwama	Nabweru	Nakaseke	Wandegeya	Bugolobi
Computers	5 (4)	5 (4)	7 (5)	22 (22)	5 (5)
Printers	1 (1)	1 (1)	2 (2)	3 (3)	2 (2)
Photocopiers	1 (1)	1 (1)	1	—	1 (1)
Telephone Lines	1 (1)	2 (2)	2 (2)	1 (1)	2 (2)
Facsimile	1	1 (1)	1 (1)	—	1
UPS	2	2	2 (2)	8 (7)	—
CD Writers	—	—	—	1 (1)	—
Speakers	5 (2)	5	3 (3)	14 (14)	3
Headphones	—	—	—	8 (4)	—
Digital Cameras	—	1 (1)	1 (1)	—	—
Projectors	2 (2)	2 (2)	1 (1)	—	—
Television Set	1 (1)	1 (1)	1 (1)	1 (1)	1 (1)
Radio	1 (1)	1 (1)	—	—	—
VCR	1	—	1 (1)	1 (1)	—
Binding Machine	—	—	—	—	2 (1)
Paper Shredder	—	—	—	—	1 (1)
Scanner	—	—	—	—	1 (1)
Generator	1 (1)	1	2 (2)	1 (1)	—
Inverters	—	—	—	—	1 (1)

Source: Survey 2001.

* Number in actual use in brackets. The table shows the facilities at the time of the survey. Unfortunately the situation in Nakaseke changed dramatically in June 2001 when the MCT suffered a fire that destroyed all but one of the computers and other electrical equipment. An international appeal was launched and some funds were raised to replace the lost equipment. About half the original numbers of computers and equipment was replaced 6 months later and the building, which suffered extensive damage, has been fully restored through local community efforts.

Equipment

There were 5–7 computers in each telecentre, with the exception of Wandegeya Cyber-Mart, which had 22 computers. Most of the computers were Pentium II clones. In Nakaseke, three of the seven computers were 486s. All facilities had at least one laser printer, one or two telephone lines, a facsimile machine, a photocopier, and a television set. All except Bugolobi had an uninterrupted power supply (UPS) and at least one overhead unit (Table 17). Except for Wandegeya, the telecentres were generally as well equipped as the cybercafés; however, the telecentres tended to have a wider array of equipment, some of which seemed to be underutilized.

Services offered

A wide variety of services were being provided to the public in the telecentres: telephone services, facsimile services, email and Internet access, library services, and training. No radio or library services were offered by the cybercafés. All the telecentres except Buwama had access to the Internet at the time of the survey early in 2001.

All facilities, except for Wandegeya Cyber-Mart, offered telephone services (see Table 18). The Buwama telecentre, whose connection was provided and maintained by the private provider MTN, was having problems sustaining telephone services on account of weak network signals. Telephone services were for both out-going and incoming calls although the latter were less frequent. Telephone charges in the Nakaseke and Buwama telecentres were lower than in Kampala. Both Telecentres had MTN lines and had received a small subsidy from the company that was passed on to customers. Call charges in Kampala were as follows: Local call (1 minute) 100 shillings (0.06 USD), long distance, 230 shillings (0.13 USD) and international call, 1450 shillings (0.81 USD). Tariffs for mobile services are higher and sensitive to congestion with peak time charges higher than for off-peak periods. MTN charges were; Call on MTN network (1 minute) 170 shillings (0.09 USD) off-peak, and 210 shillings, peak. Call to other network (1 minute) 250 shillings (0.14 USD, off-peak) and 325 shillings (0.18 USD, peak). The cost of calling a landline for the same time period was about midway between the cost of calling the same network and another mobile network.

Table 18. Services offered at each of the telecentres and cybercafés*

Service	Buwama	Nabweru	Nakaseke	Wandegeya	Bugolobi
Photocopying	✓	✓	✓	—	✓
Email	—	✓	✓	✓	✓
Internet	—	✓	✓	✓	✓
Word processing and typesetting	✓	✓	✓	✓	✓
IT Skills Training	✓	✓	✓	✓	—
Library Services	✓	✓	✓	—	—
Telephone	✓	✓	✓	—	✓
Facsimile	✓	✓	✓	—	✓
Television	✓	✓	✓	—	✓
Video Services	✓	✓	✓	—	✓
Radio	✓	✓	✓	—	—
Scanning	—	—	✓	✓	✓

Source: Survey 2001.
Note: Buwama, Nabweru, Nakaseke telecentres; Wandegeya and Bugolobi cybercafés

Pre-paid mobile telephone service charges were even higher yet these are very popular. In all the community telecentres, pre-paid phone services could be obtained from call boxes located usually on the telecentre premises on a wall outside for example. This meant that these call boxes were available to the public anytime even when the TC was officially closed.

Facsimile services were obtainable only from Nakaseke, Nabweru, and Bugolobi, which was the only facility offering Internet-based facsimile services. The facsimile services offered in Nakaseke and Nabweru were limited to East Africa. This limited coverage was a constant source of complaint by users at both sites. The telecentre staff reported that there was a huge demand for fax services to Europe and North America but did not state why these were not being offered. The Nakaseke and Nabweru telecentres had considerable technical difficulties with incoming facsimile messages but the reason for this could not be established. In Buwama, the facsimile machine had not worked since it was installed due to what the staff called 'incompatibility of technology'. All the facilities, except Bugolobi were providing skills training in basic computer familiarization and in the use of software packages such as Microsoft® Word and Excel, email and Internet applications. None of the TCs offered any technical training or technical support to customers as seen in Timbuktu MCT. All centres, except for the Wandegeya Cyber-Mart, were also providing photocopying services.

Table 19 shows that, in general, the telecentres were offering a wider range of services than the cybercafés. It is difficult to state whether this is good or bad. What seems clear is that the cybercafés appeared to have a niche for themselves and were refraining from wading into already taken territory (e.g., photocopying, which abounds in the city). The telecentres appeared to be 'jacks of all trades'. It could be argued that the telecentres had a moral imperative to be multifunctional because they were usually the only such facilities in the areas where they are located. The founding ideologies for the two types of facilities also differ markedly. Whereas the telecentres have a development, social, and economic empowerment motive, the cybercafés are primarily profit-oriented market ventures. To spread their services thinly over a wide service arena would therefore seem antithetical.

Access

Telecentre use and users

The survey findings suggest that computer use among a random sample of both potential and actual users had improved between the start of the project and the time of study. In 1999, when a baseline survey was conducted close to the start of the Buwama and Nabweru projects, only 13.6% of respondents claimed they had ever used a computer. In 2001, of the 505 respondents, 41% said they had used a computer. But less than half (44.2%) of the survey respondents were using telecentres or cybercafés (Table 19). This result shows the low use of these facilities by rural populations. Seventy-six percent of the sample stated that they use neither the telecentre nor the cybercafé and indicated that the preferred method of sending and receiving information was by word of mouth through human messengers and informers. This seems to suggest that for a large number of rural folk the telephone or newer forms of information and communication have not become commonplace. This is definitely different from the perception in Senegal where the telephone is seen as a daily tool. In contrast with the total sample, a large number of respondents in rural Nakaseke (61.1%) used the telecentre unlike in Nabweru (30.0%) and urban Bugolobi (33.3%). The Nakaseke telecentre was the most heavily used, followed by Wandegeya (55%). This pattern of usage in Wandegeya was thought to be a function of the location of the cybercafé near the Makerere University Campus because students constituted a sizeable user population.

Most of the computers in the community TCs were under utilized and the studies have suggested that usage is largely restricted to the processing of text and documents. Data from the exit poll confirms the ubiquity of the use of word processing software across most of the telecentres. Word processing was the only service offered by all five telecentres in the sample. The exception was Wandegeya, where 91.7% of its clients indicated that they had used the Internet. The high usage of Internet and email at the cybercafés (especially Wandegeya) was reinforced by the observation that all 19 visitors during the 4-day observation period used the Internet or email.

There was minimal use of computers for email or Internet in two of the three rural telecentres, and the situation did not change much between 1999 and 2001. In Buwama for instance, in 1999, 1.5% of the respondents stated they had used a computer for email and Internet. In 2001, the corresponding figure was 5.5%. The situation in urban and periurban telecentres was much different. In Bugolobi, Wandegeya, and Nabweru, the percentage of respondents who had used email once in their lives was 42.9%, 78.3%, and 42%, respectively; whereas, 17.5%, 61.8%, and 44.4% had used the Internet. The use of email and Internet services in Nabweru had clearly dramatically increased in 2 years. In 1999, the figures for email and Internet use were 6.7% and 5.1%, respectively. Poor Internet use in the rural TCs can be explained by two main reasons; poor electricity and weak and expensive connectivity. In Buwama, the cost of wireless connectivity from MTN was huge yet it was not always guaranteed because of the line-of sight requirement based on the under developed level of wireless infrastructure. Tales were told of how one had to find the best point/location usually on high ground to get or receive the best quality voice relay. In Nabweru,

Information and Communication Techonologies for Development in Africa

although the electricity situation was not as bad as in Buwama, the huge telephone bills were a constant worry. Of the three telecentres (Buwama, Nakaseke, and Nabweru), only in Nabweru was the use of email and Internet recorded. Nabweru, is located on the outskirts of Kampala and therefore has access to more developed telecommunications infrastructure. Like the entrepreneurial telecentres in Senegal, Buwama rented its generator to augment revenues.

Service use shows a concentration on telephone and television services in the rural telecentres, and on email and Internet in the urban cybercafés. In Buwama, 30% of respondents made and received their telephone calls from the telecentre, whereas 35.7% watched television in the telecentre (Table 19). In Buwama, television and video were popular for entertainment, particularly among children below 16 years of age, who represented 51.5% of all users (see Figure 5). A continuous stream of viewers was observed in the telecentre during the 4 days of data collection. The radio and audiocassettes were also a great hit in the Buwama telecentre. In rural Nakaseke, the library was by far the most popular service for both adults and children followed by photocopying and newspapers. In the course of the 4 days of data collection in Nakaseke, 76 children below the age of 16 years (54% of all visitors) came to the library. In Buwama and Nakaseke most use was made of the services on .ocation as videos or audiotapes were not usually borrowed or taken away from the centre as is common in the city.

Figure 4. Percentage use of the services offered at the three telecentres

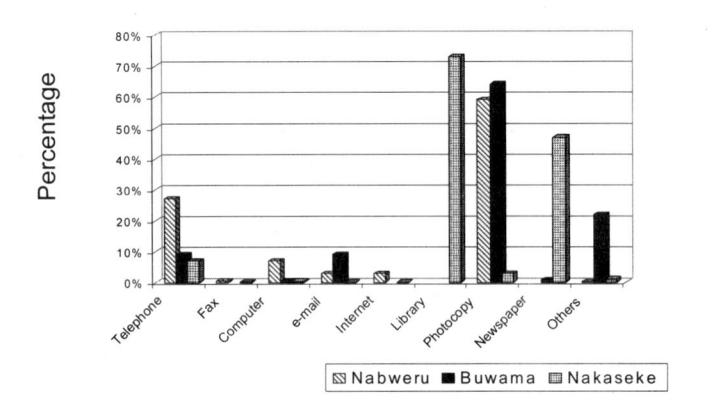

Table 19. Percentage of services used

	Bugolobi (n=99)	Wandegeya (n=100)	Nabweru (n=100)	Buwama (n=100)	Nakaseke (n=108)	Total (n=507)
Do you use a telecentre or cybercafe?						
Yes	33.3	55.0	30.0	40.0	61.1	44.2
No	66.7	45.0	70.0	60.0	38.9	55.8
Where do you make telephone calls?	(n=97)	(n=99)	(n=98)	(n=97)	(n=101)	(n=492)
Telecentre	—	—	0.3	32.0	34.7	16.1
Cybercafe	16.5	22.2	—	—	—	7.7
None	83.5	77.8	86.7	68.0	65.3	76.2
Where do you receive telephone calls?	(n=96)	(n=99)	(n=98)	(n=93)	(n=90)	(n=476)
Telecentre	—	—	6.1	24.7	15.6	9.0
Cybercafe	5.2	4.0	—	—	—	1.9
None	94.8	96.0	93.9	75.3	84.4	89.1
Where do you send faxes from?	(n=96)	(n=99)	(n=96)	(n=80)	(n=87)	(n=458)
Telecentre	—	—	7.3	—	2.3	2.0
Cybercafe	9.4	24.2	1.0	—	—	7.4
None	90.6	75.8	91.7	100	97.7	90.6
Where do you receive faxes?	(n=96)	(n=97)	(n=96)	(n=80)	(n=88)	(n=457)
Telecentre	—	—	4.2	—	2.3	1.3
Cybercafe	3.1	7.2	1.0	—	—	2.4
None	96.9	92.8	94.8	100	97.7	96.3
Where do you use email?	(n=95)	(n=99)	(n=96)	(n=92)	(n=85)	(n=465)
Telecentre	—	—	7.3	10.9	—	3.6
Cybercafé	14.7	40.4	1.0	—	1.2	12.0
None	85.3	59.6	91.7	89.1	98.8	84.4

Continued

Table 19. Continued

	Bugolobi (n=99)	Wandegeya (n=100)	Nabweru (n=100)	Buwama (n=100)	Nakaseke (n=108)	Total (n=507)
Where do you use Internet?	(n=94)	(n=99)	(n=95)	(n=91)	(n=84)	(n=463)
Telecentre	—	—	7.4	7.7	—	3.0
Cybercafe	8.5	33.3	2.1	1.1	1.2	9.7
None	91.5	66.7	90.5	91.2	98.8	87.3
Where do you listen to the radio?	(n=93)	(n=98)	(n=93)	(n=96)	(n=90)	(n=470)
Telecentre	—	—	2.2	34.4	2.2	7.9
Cybercafe	8.6	6.1	—	—	—	3.0
None	91.4	93.9	97.8	65.6	97.8	89.1
Where do you watch the TV?	(n=92)	(n=99)	(n=98)	(n=98)	(n=88)	(n=475)
Telecentre	—	—	13.3	35.7	14.8	12.8
Cybercafe	6.5	10.1	—	—	—	3.4
None	93.5	89.9	86.7	64.3	85.0	83.8
Where do you listen to audiocassettes?	(n=92)	(n=99)	(n=90)	(n=93)	(n=92)	(n=466)
Telecentre	—	—	2.2	29.0	10.9	8.4
Cybercafe	3.3	3.0	—	—	—	1.3
None	96.7	97.0	97.8	71.0	89.1	90.3
Where do you watch videos?	(n=91)	(n=99)	(n=93)	(n=96)	(n=92)	(n=471)
Telecentre	—	—	4.3	35.4	33.7	14.6
Cybercafe	3.3	8.1	—	—	—	2.3
None	96.7	91.9	95.7	64.6	66.3	83.0

Source: Survey 2001

User profiles

This study once more demonstrates that more males than females make use of telecentre facilities. The survey showed that 48.1% of the men, as compared with 39% of the women, were using all the telecentres and cybercafés at the time of the study. This trend was reaffirmed by two other sources of information, the exit poll and document analysis, which showed that women comprised about 30% or less of all users. User registration records kept by all three telecentres showed that a lower proportion of females (29.0%) were registered telecentre users. Buwama had the smallest number of registered female users (19.6%) while Nabweru had the largest (39.0%), and Nakaseke had 27.0%.

Figure 5. Men and women registered users of community telecentres

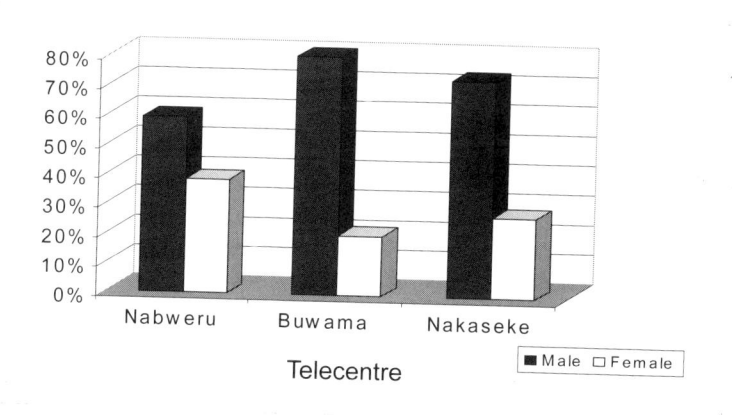

The majority of the users (71.4%) were between the ages of 18 and 50 years. Close to one-third of the users (27.1%) were children below the age of 16 years. Usage of telecentres by children was concentrated in Nakaseke on the library (54.3%) and in Buwama on watching television (51.5%). The youngest users were found in Nakaseke, and the oldest were in Buwama, which had the widest age range of users (see Figure 6). Very few old people used the telecentres and no handicapped individual was seen using any of the community telecentres in four days of continuous observation.

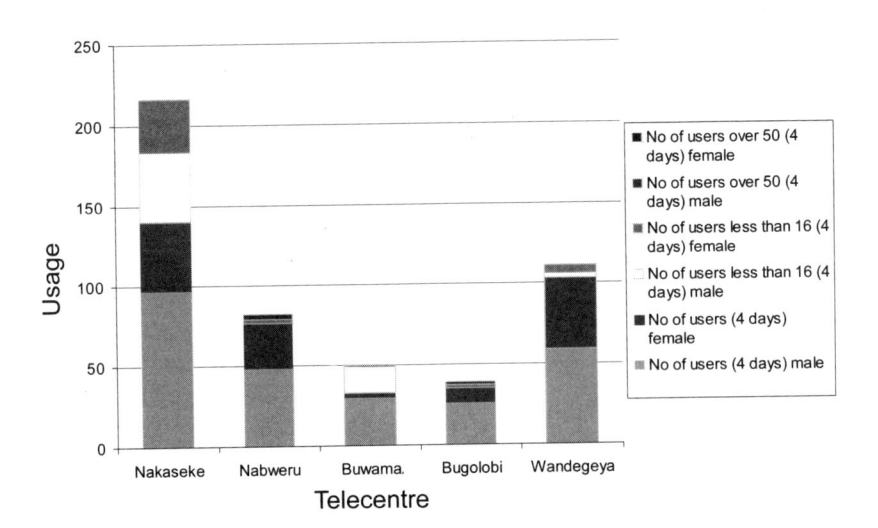

Figure 6. Observed usage of telecentres

Service delivery

The quality of service was directly related to the state of equipment and related factors such as availability of electricity and the quality of telephone connectivity. Power failures were a constant source of irritation. Several pieces of equipment at the telecentres were out of service. This is in sharp contrast to the situation in the cybercafés. Despite the fact that Wandegeya Cyber-Mart had more computers than the three telecentres combined, its computers were all working; whereas a total of 4 of 17 computers in the other telecentres were not working. A number of reasons were cited, one example being that the rural telecentres found it difficult to get urban-based technicians to help with technical problems. Another reason was the bureaucratic red tape that the telecentres were required to go through to get problems fixed usually with the project-implementing agency. Delays in equipment repair translated into unreliable and inefficient services, and compelled customers to seek other alternatives (usually in private cybercafés).

Table 20. Frequency of technical problems and how they were handled

	Buwama S	Buwama F	Nabweru S	Nabweru F	Nakaseke S	Nakaseke F	Wandegeya S	Wandegeya F	Bugolobi S	Bugolobi F
Computer crashes	Other	Twice	Other	Twice	Other	Once in 6 months	Staff	Twice	Not Stated	Not Stated
Printer break down	Staff	Thrice	Other	Never	Other	Rare	Staff	Many times	Other	Once
Software not working	Staff	Twice	Staff	Once	Staff and Others	Rare	Not stated	Not stated	Staff	Rare
Computer hardware servicing	Other	Twice	Other	Once (a year)	Other	—	Staff	Once	Staff	Rare
Supplies out	Staff	Many times	Staff	Once	Other	Rare	Staff	Depends on usage	—	—
Electrical problems	Other	Many times	Other	times	Many Other	times	Many Other	—	Other	4 times
Telephone and connectivity problems	Other	Twice	Other	Twice	Other	Many times	NA	NA	Other	Once

Source: Survey 2001 (S = solved by; F = frequency of occurrence each month).

In addition to unusable 'out of order' equipment, some other equipment were underutilized, e.g., UPS. In both Buwama and Nabweru, these had never functioned. Both telecentres had a standby generator they could use in cases of power failures, but staff in both Buwama and Nabweru indicated that the generators were rarely used because, in addition to the extra costs incurred for fuel, their power output was too low to run all of the electrical equipment. Consequently, in the case of Buwama, the generator was often hired out to generate some revenue for the telecentre. The cybercafés and the Nakaseke telecentre depended on inverters instead of generators. The inverters, unlike generators, did not consume fuel and were practically noiseless.

Telecentre staff were asked about the type and frequency of equipment-related technical problems they encountered and how they solved them. The telecentres depended more on others for solutions; whereas, the cybercafés relied on their staff to solve technical problems (Table 20). This suggests that the cybercafé staff were more technically skilled than those of the community TCs. There were frequent interruptions in electricity supplied by the Uganda Electricity Board. Telephone services also broke down fairly often and affected not only telephony but also email and Internet services. Again, the Wandegeya Cyber-Mart was an exception because it relied on wireless access technology; whereas, the other telecentres were using dial-up access to the worldwide web. Dial-up access is painfully slow and inefficient because it is prone to frequent disconnections. Bugolobi was planning to change from dial-up to wireless access, and Nabweru was dreaming of installing wireless connection/network. Buwama, which had a wireless line connection, was not altogether free from difficulties as indicated earlier.

In Buwama and Nakaseke, staff cited the long distance the technicians had to travel from Kampala to solve technical problems as a major constraint. This was costly and the equipment was sometimes damaged if it needed to be transported to Kampala for repair. The telecentre staff complained that the companies contracted to handle technical and maintenance problems were always slow to respond. Another general complaint was shoddy work done by the technicians. In many cases, the work was poor and the problems soon recurred.

The rural telecentres in Nakaseke and Buwama had the most intense connectivity problems. For a good deal of the project duration, Nakaseke and Buwama have not been able to offer email and Internet services mainly because of poor connectivity. Both telecentres are connected to their ISPs by cellular technology, but the ISPs are concentrated in central Kampala where the networks are most efficient. Rural wireless networks are being developed at a slower pace because of the physical challenges created by the terrain and the associated costs.

Power supply – i.e., electricity – was a major problem. All the TCs except Wandegeya indicated that they suffered electrical/electricity problems many times each month (Table 20) and all five facilities relied mainly on the Uganda Electricity Board for electricity. Although Buwama and Nabweru each had standby generators, they were inefficient and ineffective because of the high cost of fuel. Their power output was also too low to run all the equipment and in particular, the photocopiers, which generated the greatest revenues. The generators were therefore rarely used for the purpose for which they were intended. What this means is that whenever there was a power failure or interruption (which was and still is quite frequent), electricity-dependent services were shut down until the supply was restored. Under conditions of long power interruption, the UPS equipment was not particularly useful. Although electricity interruptions were common and frequent occurrences, users still felt frustrated by them.

- 'Power here can spend 2 days without being on so it means no business for those two days' (Nakaseke, Focus Group Discussion); and
- 'I went to the centre to make photocopies but throughout the week the photocopier was down so I decided to go to Semuto, a distance of more than 10 km away' (Kyamutakasa–Nakaseke, Focus Group Discussion).

Unlike Buwama and Nabweru, the Nakaseke telecentre and the cybercafés depended on batteries to power the systems and equipment during power failures. The batteries were said to be better than generators because they required no fuel.

Impediments to use

Several factors were cited during the focus group discussions (FGD) as being impediments to wider use of the telecentres.

- Limited range of services: It was noted that telecentre managers failed to provide an attractive range of services to capture or fully satisfy the information needs of local community members. For example, some

- FGD participants pointed out that they would have benefited from a personal announcements service on FM radio stations via the telecentres. One FGD participant commented that: 'Our kind of business is local and the people we correspond with are local, we use radio announcements. How do we benefit from the telecentre?'
- Poor location of telecentres: The FGD results indicate that the locations of all three community telecentres affected accessibility and use of the facilities. The Nabweru telecentre is located in the administrative centre of the sub-county, the same location as a police station, a prison, and the sub-county magistrate court. These three institutions are law enforcement agencies that constitute a veritable and powerful threat to some users even when they are innocent. In Buwama, the telecentre is tucked away off the main road, making it invisible and inconvenient. In comparison, the Nakaseke telecentre is on the main street, but this also creates problems. The noise from passing traffic and vehicles disturbs library users and there is no privacy for telephone users who can be seen from the road.
- Accessibility: Unlike the rural telecentres, the cybercafés were relatively easy to reach because they are located in Kampala. The cybercafés were within 500 m of 37.0% of the user's residences in Bugolobi and of 17.0% in Wandegeya. The rural telecentres in Buwama and Nakaseke were far from many of their users. In Buwama, 21.9% of the users had to travel between 1 and 5 km and 34.0% had to travel more than 5 km to reach the telecentre. The situation in Nakaseke was even worse: 47.0% had to travel between 1 and 5 km and 36.1% had to travel more than 5 km. Whereas the majority of respondents in the urban telecentre and cybercafés (41.3–65.6%) did not have to spend any money to reach the service points, in Buwama 30.0% and in Nakaseke 12.0% of users had to spend between UGS 1001–5000 (USD 1 = UGS 1700) to reach the telecentre and access the services. Some users stated this was one reason for not using the telecentres more often. Community members asserted during the focus group discussions that potential clients who did not live in the vicinity of the telecentre found it difficult to access the services, especially if they had to incur transport costs to get there and back.
- Non-functional services: Some telecentre equipment does not work for a long time due to delays in getting technicians to fix the problems or in getting supplies from Kampala. This discourages users from

returning or drives them away altogether, as seen in the views of two FGD participants: 'I went to the centre (Nakaseke) to make photocopies but throughout the week the photocopier was down so I decided to go to Semuto trading centre; At times the computers don't function properly, the mouse sometimes refuses to work.'

During a monitoring visit to Nabweru in October 2000, it was observed that the printer was not being used and had not functioned for more than 1 week because 'there was no **cartridge**'. It was found that the telecentre was waiting for the implementing agency, the Uganda National Council for Science and Technology, to authorize the purchase and supply of the cartridges.

- Poor publicity of telecentre services: There was not a great degree of awareness about the telecentres, especially in Nabweru. Twenty-seven percent of respondents had no knowledge of the existence of the Nabweru telecentre. A further 27.0% who knew of the telecentre did not know how far it was from their homes. It is not clear if this was due to poor publicity of the telecentre and its services, or simply symptomatic of city life where alternatives abound and anomie a way of life. Some FGD participants felt that this was due to failures in publicity and sensitization. The discussants suggested that this could be remedied through outreach, sensitization seminars, and advertisement in both the electronic (radio) and print media.
- Privacy: In practically all the facilities there was little privacy, especially when using the telephones. This observation was affirmed during the FGDs when it was pointed out that:
  The arrangement of the telecentre does not allow us to feel free, for example where the phone is placed, you can never talk anything confidential unless you tell the receptionist to go out. At times you would want to quarrel with someone on the phone, but you cannot when everybody around is listening.
- Inconvenient hours: The community (Nakaseke, Buwama, and Nabweru) telecentres keep public, i.e., government 8-hour days. This severely limits the times when the facilities are open to the public. The telecentres do not operate at night, on Sundays, or during public holidays. Yet these are precisely the times when more people might wish to use the facilities. The cybercafés are open longer.

- Cost of services: Although FGD participants found it difficult to suggest reasonable and affordable charges for the various services, they felt that telecentres ought to charge lower rates than the market. The reason for this feeling among community members was their perception of the telecentres as community projects. This same view was expressed during the baseline survey of 1999. Some of the FGD participants claimed that:
  The cost of computer training is unaffordable, for instance 'Introduction to Computers' is UGS 15,000 and by the time you finish about four packages you will have spent something like UGS 150,000. The cost of services is a bit high, and yet some of us stay very far, which means adding transport expenses on what you pay for the services ... The rates should be reduced given the income of the people around.
- Poor management: The Buwama telecentre had suffered from interminable management difficulties, which have had a negative impact on service delivery. There had been disagreements among the staff and between the staff and the local management committee, which affected the smooth running of the TC. One fine day the manager simply absconded, but mercifully without taking any of the equipment!

These difficulties were said to have been largely due to the absence of guidelines specifying the roles and responsibilities of the staff and the local management committee.

Relevance

To examine relevance, users were asked why they used the telecentres and cybercafés. The main reason for which more than half of the users visited the telecentres and cybercafés was social – to maintain contact with family members and friends. The use of the telephone for social reasons was much higher in rural telecentres (Buwama 77.4% and Nakaseke 63.9%) than in the cybercafés. However, the use of facsimile, email, and Internet for social contacts was higher in the cybercafés than in the telecentres. In Wandegeya, 54.2% used facsimile, 62.5% email, and 36.4% the Internet to communicate with friends and family members compared with only one respondent in Nakaseke who used email and Internet for the same purpose. The findings presented in Table 21 suggest that ICTs were more relevant for social activities than for development-oriented action. The most prevalent purpose for making and receiving telephone calls, or sending and receiving faxes and email was social – for contacting family and friends. Between 1.0 and 20.0% of users visited the TCs for business or commercial reasons. Over 50% visited the TCs for entertainment yet very few visits were made to the same TCs in search of government information.

Information needs expressed by community members placed education and the acquisition of new skills topmost followed by health information, production information, and information about governance and government information. However, the communities preferred sources for this information were often not the telecentres. An analysis of the sources of information used by community members revealed a high dependence on sources external to the telecentres or cybercafés, although the telecentres fared better than the cybercafés in this regard.

Table 21. Purpose of last visit (expressed as percentages)*

	Bugolobi	Wandegeya	Nabweru	Buwama	Nakaseke	Total
Making telephone call:	(n=16)	(n=22)	(n=15)	(n=31)	(n=36)	(n=120)
Social: family/friends	31.3	50	53.3	77.4	63.9	52.9
Education/training	18.8	22.7	—	6.5	11.1	11.7
Health	12.5	4.5	—	3.2	5.6	5.0
Business/commercial	31.3	18.0	46.7	12.9	16.7	21.7
Emergency	6.3	4.5	—	—	2.8	2.5
Receiving telephone call:	(n=5)	(n=4)	(n=7)	(n=23)	(n=15)	(n=54)
Social: family/friends	40.0	50.0	28.6	60.9	60.0	53.7
Education/training	20.0	—	14.3	21.7	21.7	16.7
Health	20.0	—	—	4.3	4.3	3.7
Business/commercial	20.0	50.0	42.9	13.0	3.0	24.1
Government info	—	—	14.3	—	—	1.9
Sending facsimile:	(n=9)	(n=24)	(n=8)	—	(n=2)	(n=43)
Social: family/friends	55.6	54.2	37.5	—	50.0	51.2
Education/training	—	25.0	2.5	—	50.0	18.6
Health	—	12.5	—	—	—	7.0
Business/commercial	33.3	4.2	50.0	—	—	18.6
Government info	11.1	4.2	—	—	—	4.7

Table 21. Continued

	Bugolobi	Wandegeya	Nabweru	Buwama	Nakaseke	Total
Receiving facsimile:	(n=3)	(n=8)	(n=5)	—	(n=2)	(n=18)
Social: family/friends	—	75.0	60.0	—	50.0	55.6
Education/training	—	12.5	—	—	50.0	1.1
Business/commercial	66.7	12.5	20.0	—	—	22.2
Government info.	33.3	—	20.0	—	—	11.
Sending email:	(n=14)	(n=40)	(n=8)	(n=10)	(n=1)	(n=73)
Social: family/friends	57.1	62.5	62.5	40.0	—	57.5
Education/training	2.4	20.0	—	20.0	100	19.2
Health	—	5.0	—	10.0	—	4.1
Business/commercial	21.4	10.0	12.5	30.0	—	15.1
Entertainment	—	2.5	12.5	—	—	2.7
Other	—	—	12.5	—	—	1.4
Using Internet:	(n=8)	(n=33)	(n=9)	(n=8)	(n=1)	(n=59)
Social: family/friends	2.5	36.4	22.2	25.0	100	30.5
Education/training	37.5	30.3	2.2	—	—	25.4
Health	—	3.0	—	37.5	—	6.8
Business/commercial	12.5	6..0	11.1	37.5	—	11.9
Government Info.	12.5	3.0	—	—	—	3.4
News	12.5	9.1	—	—	—	6.8
Sports	—	—	11.0	—	—	1.7
Entertainment	12.5	12.1	33.3	—	—	13.6
Listening to radio:	(n=7)	(n=5)	(n=4)	(n=33)	(n=2)	(n=51)
Social: family/friends	—	20.0	50.0	24.2	—	19.6
Education/training	—	—	—	3.0	—	3.9
Health	—	—	—	3.0	—	2.0
Government Info.	—	—	25.0	—	—	2.0
News	14.3	—	25.0	27.3	—	21.6
Sports	—	—	—	3.0	—	2.0
Entertainment	71.4	80.0	—	39.4	100	47.1
Emergency	14.3	—	—	—	—	2.0

* Purpose for which the users employed the services the last time they used them at the telecentres (in Nabweru, Buwama, and Nakaseke) and cybercafés (in Bugolobi and Wandegeya)

Table 21. Continued

	Bugolobi	Wandegeya	Nabweru	Buwama	Nakaseke	Total
Watching television: (n=6)	(n=9)	(n=13)	(n=35)	(n=13)	(n=76)
Social: family/friends	—	—	7.7	5.7	—	3.9
Education/training	—	—	23.1	8.6	23.1	0.8
Health	—	—	—	5.7	—	2.6
Business/commercial	—	—	—	—	7.7	1.3
News	—	—	—	22.9	7.7	11.1
Sports	—	—	30.8	2.9	23.1	10.5
Entertainment	100	100	38.5	54.3	30.8	56.6
Other	—	—	—	—	7.7	1.3

* Purpose for which the users employed the services the last time they used them at the telecentres (in Nabweru, Buwama, and Nakaseke) and cybercafés (in Bugolobi and Wandegeya).

Focus group discussions show that the communities served by the telecentres appreciated the services on offer and expressed happiness that the services had been brought close to them. This was especially true of the rural telecentres of Buwama and Nakaseke, where such services did not exist before the projects.

> 'The telecentre has exposed us to what we did not know before. Like I did not know that the photocopier would enlarge or narrow what you want to photocopy '(Bongole–Buwama Focus Group Discussion).
> 'Before a photocopier was brought we used to go to Mitala Maria, 3 km away, to photocopy' (Mbizzinya–Buwama Focus Group Discussion).
> 'Some people did not know about computers but have seen and learnt about them and even bought theirs after copying ideas from the telecentre' (Nakaseke Focus Group Discussion).

Table 22. Where there is no telecentre*

	Buwama (n=17)	Nabweru (n=24)	Nakaseke (n=24)	Wandegeya (n=24)	Bugolobi (n=24)	Total (n=113)
What respondent would have done if telecentre/ cybercafe did not exist:						
Nothing	—	12.5	25	20.8	—	12.4
Do not know	11.8	16.7	8.3	8.3	—	8.8
Use other facilities	58.8	37.5	8.3	70.8	87.5	52.2
Travel to another town with same facilities	29.4	33.3	58.3	—	12.5	26.5
If other facilities, how much would same service cost?						
More than at the TC	52.9	72.2	84.0	6.3	4.3	43.0
Less than at the TC	—	—	15.8	12.5	4.3	6.5
Same as at TC	47.1	27.8	—	81.3	91.3	50.5
How far would respondent have to go to get other Service?	47.1	68.4	5.3	100	11.1	40.2
Less than 5km	—	31.6	10.5	—	11.1	12.2
6–10 km	—	—	5.3	—	—	1.2
11–15 km	—	—	5.3	—	—	1.2
16–20 km	52.9	—	73.7	—	—	28.0
More than 20 km	—	—	—	—	77.8	17.1
Not Applicable						

Source: Survey 2001.

*Alternatives (expressed as percentage) for access to the services available at the telecentres and cybercafés.

Further evidence of the importance that the communities attach to the telecentres is reflected in the proportion of respondents at the exit polls who would have had no alternative if the telecentres did not exist. Almost a third of the users in Nakaseke (33.3%) and Nabweru (29.2%) had either no alternate location or did not know where else to obtain the services they had received from the telecentre. Considered as a group, 52.2% of those polled as they exited the facilities, said that they would switch to other telecentres or cybercafés if the ones they were now using did not exist. In Nakeseke, 73.7% of the users would have had to travel over 20 km to obtain the same services, and they pointed out that the cost of these services would have been higher than at the telecentre. The cost of using alternate services in Buwama and Nabweru would also have been higher, but in the city the alternatives were easily and cheaply available.

Participants in the focus group discussions were asked about the direct benefits they received from the use of telecentres and cybercafés. These benefits included ease of communication; savings in money and time; being able to duplicate things (photocopying) quickly and cheaply; access to various types of information, especially on modern techniques of farming; knowledge of happenings in the rest of the world through reading newspapers; job advertisements for community members (volunteers); the acquisition of new skills through computer training; processing documents; and access to global information through the world wide web. In Buwama, most participants singled out the entrepreneurial-skills development seminars organized at the telecentres and conducted by the NGO 'Council for the Economic Empowerment of Women in Africa' as having been of particular significance:

> The telecentre conducts seminars that teach about good farming methods, rearing animals, poultry, crafts, business, and bookkeeping. These are of great benefit to the community (Jalamba–Buwama, Focus Group Discussion). Through the seminars, women have come to learn from one another and how to improve on what they do (Bongole–Buwama, Focus Group Discussion).

In Nakaseke, the library service was rated very highly by focus group participants:

> The library has helped many students especially those who stay near. Other members of the community go there to read newspapers, and

children go there to play computer games and watch videos. The services are not discriminatory, they cater for all ages both young and old, men and women alike (Nakaseke, Focus Group Discussion).

The individual case studies conducted at all telecentre and cybercafé sites indicated that these facilities had significant impacts on the lives of some of the users:

- 'After watching a telecentre videotape on maize growing in Tanzania where the soil is hard and rocky, I was challenged because the soil here is better. I embarked on a serious program of improving my crop quality and quantity. Since then, I have experienced an increase in both the quality and quantity of my maize produce, which has helped me improve on my income and feed my family. My maize garden is very productive and almost a model to other farmers in the area' (Steven Kityo, Buwama).
- 'With the knowledge I acquired through watching videotapes at the telecentre, I now use modern farming practices in my banana plantation. I use the right spacing between plants and crops, apply the right amounts of fertilizers, and mulch the soil to allow water retention and prevent soil erosion. At first, I didn't try these methods because I thought they would not lead to better yields ... but I am happy now ... I don't have to spend money to buy food for the family anymore' (Mr. Katwele Kintu, the Local Council II Chairman, Mbizzinnya Parish, Buwama).
- 'Before I attended computer lessons at the telecentre, I was using the free hand style to design my work. This was taking a lot of time and was not very neat. When the telecentre started, I enrolled for computer lessons in word-processing and Excel. With this knowledge, I can now make my designs on the computer. The computer knowledge has helped me improve on the quality of my work and has made my work faster and easier. This has also increased my clientele base ... Besides the computer, I use the photocopier to photocopy documents ... At times I make designs which are too big for the space on the material, and I reduce them using the photocopying machine ... These days we also just call (our suppliers in Kampala using the telecentre phone) and give them specifications of the goods we need. The suppliers collect the money from our local taxi drivers to whom they give the goods. This has saved the business money and time that would have been

incurred on transport' (Ms Namayanja Joyce, a resident of Nakaseke who designs school badges, banners, and signposts).

The exit poll data showed that 55.6% of the respondents reported that learning to use a computer had made a difference in their lives. Two direct benefits were savings in time and money (60.8%) and the capacity to process their own work independently (35.3%). A respondent in Wandegeya found a job as a result of having learnt how to use computers at the cybercafé, and sixteen respondents were hopeful about getting good jobs after their training in computers. The question is not simply whether or not these expectations are realistic, but that they give hope and the possibility of a new occupation.

Content development

It is no secret that a large chunk of the content available on the World Wide Web is of North American and European origin. Some estimates put the figure at over 90%. African content, i.e., content generated by Africans or from the continent is said to constitute less than 2% of the World Wide Web. An early and important task and challenge for the telecentres was the provision and creation of content with local appeal and relevance. This is not an easy challenge. Unlike the cybercafés, the telecentres had made some attempts to create local content. Most of these were largely directed at repackaging available information converting it from one form into another, such as in the production of videos from secondary textual material. The manager of the Wandegeya Cyber-Mart affirmed that they had not put any investment into creating local content because in his words 'we don't think it would be profitable'. The three telecentres had created mainly print materials (e.g., handouts, handbills or posters) on a limited number of subjects in agriculture and health etc. Staff members at Nakaseke TC had made a few videos on agriculture, business, and health at the time of the investigation and a directory of useful websites and newspaper cuttings of important events in the country had also been developed and kept in files mainly for reference.

Attempts by the telecentres to repackage information to suit local requirements and environments were not extensive and examples of actual content creation though limited show that efforts in this direction can have dividends. In Nabweru, information on modern agricultural methods had been collected and repackaged into posters. This information had been gathered from many institutions and sources: research institutions in Kawanda (Agricultural Research Institute); farmers associations such as the Uganda National Farmers Association (UNFA) and the Kampala District Farmers Association (KADIFA); the Ministry of Health; the AIDS Information Centre; the National Chamber of Commerce; the British Council; Straight Talk (an NGO); and the Naguru Teenage Centre.

The major challenges identified in the content development endeavour were the absence of funds, lack of relevant skills and expertise, and meaningful cost recovery among poor peasant populations. Pilot content-creation activities are being conducted outside of the telecentres, but with the telecentres as collaborators and beneficiaries. One project currently being implemented by the National Agricultural Research Organization in collaboration with the three community TCs has produced six videos mainly on agriculture and over one dozen posters (see www.agricinfo.ug). Another such example is the CD-ROM titled 'Rural Women in Africa: Ideas for Earning Money', which has become a big hit nationally and internationally. The project created a multi-media CD-ROM, which targeted women because the pictures emerging of TC use showed that they were not using the telecentre facilities as much as was expected.

The strategy involved creating a product specifically targeted at women (poor and neo or illiterate women in particular). This product responded to one of a number of primary questions raised by the women themselves during meetings to discuss the project; "How can I make more money?" Following a sequence of collaborative meetings, discussions, data/ information collection/gathering, writing, rewriting and editing, the International Women's Tribune Centre, New York, researchers, and IT experts in Kampala created/produced an interactive audio-enabled CD-ROM. The CD-ROM entitled "Rural Women in Africa: Ideas for Earning Money" features real-life stories of women Ugandan who have successfully started and run small businesses. Using the stories as starting points, practical business information and other business ideas are presented in the CD-ROM. The CD-ROM is in English and Luganda a popular Ugandan language spoken in and around Kampala and the telecentres.

The CD-ROM is immensely popular in the communities around the telecentres initially with women where it has created a huge pull towards the MCT. 'Women now line up at the telecentres to use the computers because of the CD-ROM' and a seventy-year old widow is making national and international news as a computer teacher on account of her dexterity with the CD-ROM and the accompanying hard copy "computer book", which she uses to teach others in the sub-county. The CD-ROM can be viewed at www.wougnet.org/news/cdupdate.html

Ownership, management, and sustainability

A major debate concerning telecentres and public access points in general is the issue of financial sustainability. Are they viable enough to run on their own steam? The market speaks! Closely related to the question of sustainability are those of ownership and management. Who owns the telecentre and how is it managed? These are believed to contribute in really tangible ways to financial sustainability.

At the time of the investigations, Buwama and Nabweru TCs like the other community TCs were running their operations almost exclusively on donor funds. Nakaseke had started meeting some of its operational costs, but still depended heavily on donor funding. The big question, and a source of collective anxiety for the local implementers and to some extent also for the donors, was: what would happen when the projects reach their final termination dates? Projects by their very nature are designed for finite periods, say two, three or four years, at the end of which they must come to an end or their cycle renewed. The telecentre projects reported in this chapter were designed for three years initially and they were on the third year of operations when these investigations were conducted and by that time issues of the future nature of funding (and sustainability) were on their minds and agenda.

The TCs were managed by staff members who were supervised by local management committees on one hand and the respective institutions that acted as project implementers on the other. The nature of management arrangements characterized by overlapping and sometimes unclear roles and responsibilities left much to be desired. At the telecentre level, the absence of services and price listings, timetables for service delivery or systematic organization of service delivery were suggestive of poor organizational efficiency. Among members of staff and the local management committees there was little formal training or technical skills. It was observed that more thought seemed to have been given to services and their delivery in the two TCs where men were the managers. But the fact that the one TC with a woman manager had drawn out discord between the management/steering committee and the manager makes a conclusion in respect of gender and management difficult.

Staffing

Staffing is directly related to sustainability because too large a work force can drain resources – and too few staff can be ineffective. There was, on average, a total of six staff members responsible for day-to-day operations at each of the telecentres and cybercafés. The Nakaseke telecentre and Wandegeya Cyber-Mart had the highest number of staff (eight each). There was a total of 20 staff members in the five facilities investigated 9 of whom were women. There was no significant difference in the gender distribution of staff. Only in Buwama TC was there a gender imbalance where only one staff member was a man (Table 24). Unlike the cybercafés, the telecentres depended quite heavily on volunteers who served mostly as ICT trainers or guides. The volunteers, who generally had secondary school certificates, were paid a small monthly allowance to meet some of their expenses (e.g., transport and lunch). The volunteers were usually trained at the TCs and used the opportunity of being in the TC to improve their personal skills and employability. Most of the salaried employees had diplomas or degrees in subject areas other than engineering or computer science and although some courses had been arranged for them e.g., in basic computer hardware and software most of them did not have significant technical qualifications, expertise or skills.

Each of the community telecentres had an information officer; whereas, neither of the cybercafés had such a staff position. Buwama had an additional position, a Senior Operations Officer. There were other staffing differences between the telecentres and the cybercafés. There were generally more female staff in the cybercafés, and the cybercafés had managing directors instead of managers (Table 23).

Table 23. Staffing patterns at telecentres and cybercafés
(M = male, F = female)

	Buwama	Nabweru	Nakaseke	Wandegeya	Bugolobi
Salaried staff					
Telecentre Manager	1 F	1 M	1 M	1 M	—
Assistant Telecentre Manager	—	—	1 M	1 F	—
Information Officer	1 F	1 M	1 F	—	—
Assistant Information Officer	—	—	1 F	—	—
Senior Operations Officer	1 F	—	—	—	—
ICT Trainers, Guides, and Secretaries	—	—	—	3 F, 2 M	3 F, 1 M
Total (Salaried)	3 F	2 M	4 (2 M, 2 F)	7 (3 M, 4 F)	4 (3 F, 1 M)
Volunteers					
ICT Trainers, Guides, and Secretaries	1 M, 1 F	1 M, 2 F	3 M, 1 F	—	—
Managing Director	—	—	—	1 F	1 M
Total (Volunteers)	2 (1 M, 1 F)	3 (1 M, 2 F)	4 (3 M, 1 F)	—	—
Grand Total	5 (1 M, 4 F)	5 (3 M, 2 F)	8 (5 M, 3 F)	8 (3 M, 5 F)	5 (3 F, 2 M)

Source: Survey 2001.

Community participation

Unlike the cybercafés, whose operations were supervised and directed by a managing director, the community telecentres were supervised by local management committees, which were also called steering committees. The committees in both Buwama and Nabweru were charged with similar responsibilities – advising and overseeing telecentre operations. They were made up of community members who represented different community interests or groups. The local steering committee in Buwama consisted of thirteen members, whereas, in Nabweru, the local management committee had eight members, two of whom were women. In Nabweru, committee members represented the parishes in the sub-county. However, representation in Buwama was less clear because the criteria for member selection were not clear, and not all parishes in the sub-county were represented.

Unlike in Buwama and Nabweru, Nakaseke had three different committees. There was a management committee, a local steering committee, and a core-user group committee. Each of the three committees had clearly defined roles and responsibilities that were spelled out in the terms of reference for the project. The local steering committee in Nakaseke comprised mostly local (Uganda based) representatives of the donor agencies involved in the project, such as UNESCO, IDRC, UTL, and the National Library Board. Although their role was expressly stated as 'concerned with technical issues', it was difficult to distinguish their role from that of the management committee. The management committee was charged with responsibility for policy matters and consisted of high-ranking representatives from the various stakeholder groups including UTL, UNESCO, and IDRC. The core-user group committee was made up of local community members who were users and potential users of the telecentre services (e.g., farmers, traders, doctors, and youth). Their major responsibilities were: to articulate the information and communication needs of the community; to voice community concerns and views about the telecentre and services provided; and to liaise with telecentre staff for the benefit of the community. There had been no change in the original composition of the committees since their inception, despite wishes to the contrary that had been expressed by many community members (especially in Buwama).

In terms of committee involvement in telecentre management, committee members in Buwama and Nabweru did not have the power to hire or fire staff. In Nakaseke, the local management committee could hire and fire technical staff, and the sub-county authorities could do the same with support staff, such as the cleaners and security guards because this was their contribution to the telecentre. As in Nakaseke, the sub-county authorities in Nabweru and Buwama were responsible for providing security at the telecentres. The Uganda National Council of Science and Technology (UNCST) the project implementation agency, hired all other staff members for Buwama and Nabweru. The role of the management and steering committees was restricted to recommending who could be hired or fired.

However, the committee chair or an assistant usually represented local management and steering committees when important decisions were made by UNCST about the TCs. In comparison, the managing directors of the cybercafés had absolute powers to hire and fire their employees.

The chairpersons (men) of the management or steering committees in Buwama and Nabweru were co-signatories to their respective telecentre bank accounts along with the telecentre managers. Other committee members were not involved with decisions about telecentre finances, they were simply informed from time to time about the financial performance of the telecentres and were not involved in making or approving telecentre budgets (see Table 24). UNCST, the project-implementing agency was solely responsible for the budgets of the two telecentres and for all financial assessments, including auditing of financial records.

Table 24. Nature of community involvement in management of community telecentres

Community involvement	Buwama	Nabweru	Nakaseke
Recruitment of staff	No	No	Yes
Supervision of staff	Yes	Yes	Yes
Provision of resources	Yes	Yes	Yes
Determination of prices for services	No	No	Yes

Source: Survey 2001.

In Nakaseke, the local management committee was responsible for approving the telecentre budgets. Initially, the committee was responsible for most of the purchases. At the time of the study, however, the telecentre manager was responsible for making quarterly budget estimates, which were then approved by the committee. The committee was also responsible for financial audits. However, the local steering committee remained responsible for approving the routine day-to-day expenditures incurred from the telecentre revenues. The manager had the power to spend some of the money made by the telecentre as long as the expenditure was approved by the steering committee. The level of community participation as represented by the nature of involvement of the local and management committee members in telecentre affairs appeared to be higher in Nakaseke than in Nabweru and Buwama.

Community participation in Nakaseke was greater for a number of telecentre activities. Community members were involved in the recruitment of staff, the supervision of telecentre activities, the provision of financial and material resources, and the determination of prices for telecentre services (Table 25). In Buwama and Nabweru, community involvement was restricted to the supervision of telecentre activities and the provision of supplementary resources.

The local communities made significant contributions to all of the telecentres. All three telecentres were housed in public or community facilities, and the premises were provided free of charge. The Buwama telecentre was housed in a centre constructed for the community by World Vision. Nakaseke TC was occupying a community hall while Nabweru was housed in three rooms in the local council offices. In addition to providing premises and security, local authorities also provided furniture.

The opinion was pervasive in Nakaseke, as in the other telecentres, that the current management model would not ensure sustainability. It was pointed out that the relative success of the Nakaseke telecentre had depended a lot on the goodwill and commitment of local political leaders. These leaders had made tremendous contributions toward community mobilization, particularly during the initial stages of the project. There was local concern that if the political leadership was not maintained following the general elections, the telecentre might be adversely affected. One member of the local management committee in Nakaseke observed:

> ... the most important factor in determining the success or failure of any business is the charisma and the level of entrepreneurship of its managers. I have seen many privately owned secretarial bureaus spring up only to close a few months later. This is all because of poor management and lack of entrepreneurial skills.

In Nabweru, the chair of the local management committee suggested that the management arrangement should continue because 'it creates employment for community members,' but he admitted that things were not working well and there was talk of contracting out the telecentre. However, he was unsure of the position of the committee because it had not met for at least 8 months.

The situation in Buwama, was even less clear as the local management committee had been embroiled in endless wrangles with the staff, with the result that the committee had distanced itself from the telecentre until 'the mess is sorted out'. The Acacia Project Officer reflected:

> ... If I were to start this project all over again, I would definitely prefer to have the telecentres run like typical business enterprises right from the beginning ... Also, from the word go, I would involve the local administration (Local Councils) in the implementation of the project.

Telecentre ownership

All the committee members interviewed stated that the telecentres belonged to the communities and that the donors and the implementing agencies (UNCST, in the cases of Buwama and Nabweru) were only there to give a helping hand in the short term before the communities took full control of the projects. The projects have always been described and labelled as community projects. How could the communities be said to own the telecentres if they could not recruit staff or set prices? The local committee members believed that the communities would own the facilities at the end of the project and this was enough reason to label them as they did – i.e., as belonging to the community. However if ownership confers a degree of control, then it would be fair to say that the local Buwama and Nabweru communities did not own the telecentres, the UNCST owned them. The UNCST was an absentee owner or a trustee as was the National Commission for UNESCO for the Nakaseke TC.

Cash matters

A significant dimension of sustainability is profit. Discussions with management staff of all five facilities confirmed that they were recording income, although none of the facilities was generating enough money to cover all their needs.

There was a significant difference in expenditure patterns between the telecentres and the cybercafés. Table 26 presents responses to the question 'what expenditures are you responsible for?' In Nabweru and Buwama the telecentre staff did not spend money on any of the identified expenditure items. They had no authority to incur expenditure whatsoever.

Staff at all the telecentres disclosed that, according to telecentre policy, they were supposed to bank all proceeds from the sale of products and services. Donor funds were used by the implementing agencies, the UNCST and National Commission for UNESCO, to cover all expenditures, except in emergencies, such as when there were delays in accessing cash from the project implementing agencies. Project policy stipulated predetermined levels of expenditure for Nabweru and Buwama. For example, they were not supposed to spend more than UGS 80,000 on stationery or UGS 100,000 (1700=1USD) on the telephone each month. Staff in Buwama and Nabweru complained about this policy and pointed out that it made them appear ineffective and inefficient because they could not spend above certain limits, although this was often necessary. They argued for example that for telephone and photocopying services that were hugely popular the restrictions on spending had a negative affect on the provision of these services.

Table 25. Staff responsibility for expenditures (na = not applicable)

	Buwama	Nabweru	Nakaseke	Wandegeya	Bugolobi
Operating costs	–	–	partial	yes	yes
Equipment *replacement	–	–	no	yes	yes
*maintenance	–	–	no	yes	yes
Tarrifs telephone, water & electricity	–	–	yes	yes	yes
Salaries	–	–	yes	yes	yes
Allowances (committee & volunteers)	–	–	yes	na	na
Overtime	–	–	yes	yes	no
Outreach prog.	–	–	yes	yes	no
Advertising costs	–	–	partial	no	no

Source: Survey 2001.

Photocopying, telephone services, and computer training were the highest earners for those facilities that offered these services (Table 26). Profits and sometimes charges varied from one facility to the other. The Bugolobi Business Centre, for example, made 100% profit on photocopying, but Nabweru lost money on the same service. In Nabweru, the biggest customer for photocopying services was the local administration, which took a long time to settle the bills, and sometimes never did. Nakaseke was making sizeable profits on telephone services, but this was related to the fact that telephone services were subsidized in Nakaseke but not in Nabweru and Buwama. Only the Wandegeya Cyber-Mart reported profits for email and Internet services. Staff at the cybercafés lamented that email and Internet business used to be very profitable, but that profits were falling and they could now barely break even because the numbers of clients had declined due to stiff competition from the many new cybercafés in Kampala. Wandegeya Cyber-Mart was consequently considering slashing its Internet charges from UGS 100 to only UGS 50 per minute. The email and Internet service at Nabweru was losing money not because of competition, but because of low demand.

Despite claims that all telecentres were making profits and the assertions by staff that they would be interested in setting up similar businesses themselves if they had the capital, the figures on revenue flows are not convincing. For 12 of the 18 months for which data were available, the monthly income would not have adequately covered the monthly salary of the telecentre manager (UGS 425,000=USD 250). The overall trend showed a decline in telecentre incomes. It is intriguing that telecentre staff would declare interest in starting telecentre businesses unless they believed in their viability. If this was the case, why then were the telecentres not doing better? Assuming that there was no financial impropriety in operations, and there is little reason to believe there was, the answer might lie in the management model. The private cybercafés, which were not in any way subsidized and were located in areas characterized by stiff competition, were making a profit or at least managing to break even from one month to the next (see Table 26).

Information and Communication Techonologies for Development in Africa

Table 26. Estimated monthly income and expenditures (in UGS) by service type
(SNA = service not available, NS = not stated, 1USD=1700)

	Buwama Income	Buwama Cost	Nabweru Income	Nabweru Cost	Nakaseke Income	Nakaseke Cost	Wandegeya Income	Wandegeya Cost	Bugolobi Income	Bugolobi Cost
Photocopying	70,000	20,000	120,000	122,000	141,000	42,000	SNA	SNA	550,000	280,000
Document processing	40,000	—	NS	NS	8,000	1,000	SNA	SNA	400,000	160,000
Telephone	150,000	100,000	280,000	200,000	150,000	20,000	SNA	SNA	SNA	SNA
Video shows	2,400	—	—	—	—	—	SNA	SNA	SNA	SNA
Generator rental	15,000	—	SNA	SNA	SNA	SNA	SNA	SNA	SNA	SNA
Library services	—	—	—	—	20,000	15,000	SNA	SNA	SNA	SNA
Computer training	35,000	10,000	200,000	40,000	120,000	90,000	100,000	NS	SNA	SNA
Email and Internet	SNA	SNA	32,000	100,000 (ISP)	SNA	SNA	2 million	1.785 million	300,000	500,000
Facsimile	SNA	SNA	500	NS	3,000	6,000	SNA	SNA	NS	NS
Outreach	NS	NS	NS	NS	—	70,000	SNA	SNA	SNA	SNA

Source: Survey 2001

Conclusion

The testimonies of ordinary people indicate that telecentres have made a significant difference in the lives of Ugandans, especially but not exclusively for those living in the rural areas where the TCs are located. The nature and degree of impact has been slight for some, yet fundamental for others. The question is not if there has been change, but rather how much change of the desired type has occurred and whether this change will last. For the good and desirable change to last, the telecentres will have to receive continued support. Differences observed between the private cybercafés and the community TCs suggest some dimensions of the required changes that might make community telecentres more sustainable. Or is it perhaps as the evolutionary thesis suggests that it is only a matter of time?

These telecentre projects were exploratory, experimental, and had a short life-span. Although all of them were still being implemented at the time of the investigations, they were in their dying days as donor-funded projects awaiting imminent transformation to more permanent status and possibly changed ownership. Two of the TCs, Buwama and Nabweru, have since December 2002 been taken over by the local administration and their fate is to some extent uncertain. However, it is evident that the TCs have given men, women, and children a taste of some of the contemporary tools of information and communication common to the developed world. The projects have shown that the isolation of rural communities can be broken. But more remains to be learnt and done if the experiment with telecentres is to achieve the expectations for universal and affordable access to all community groups in rural Africa.

Chapter 6

Telecentres in South Africa

Straddling the southern tip of the continent, South Africa occupies 1.2 million km². Since 1994, and the official end of apartheid, a democratic government led by the ANC has attempted to share and spread the riches of the country to a wider majority of the people. Approximately 48% of the 42 million people live in poverty (under ZAR 1000 or USD 83 a month). South Africa remains a divided society, with the white community (11% of the total population) generally living affluently, whereas most of the black African population (72% of the total population) live in poverty. Fifty-eight percent of households have electricity, 45% have water taps inside their homes, and 34% of households have a telephone.

The focus of the telecentre research was the Northern Province, which had been identified by the Government of South Africa as a development priority area that was in dire need of communication services. Six telecentres in the area were selected for the study: Botlokwa, Phalala, Makuleke, Mankweng, Bakgaga-ba-Mothapo, and Thakgalane. The research was conducted between March and October 2000 and involved, in addition to 7–10 days of field research in each study site, a training workshop, and local and provincial feedback and dissemination workshops.

Telecommunications context

South Africa has by far the largest number of fixed line (estimated to be 4.9 million in 2002) and mobile connections in Africa and the most advanced information and communication technology (ICT) sector on the continent with nearly three million Internet accounts in 2001. However, access to ICTs in South Africa tends to follow lines of existing inequalities, which are quite wide because of the legacy of apartheid.

The Telecommunications Act was enacted in 1996 and declared universal access to telephony as the cornerstone of government policy. The Telecommunications Act created the Independent Communications Authority of South Africa (ICASA) in July 2000, which resulted from the merger of the South African Telecom Regulatory Authority (SATRA) and the Independent Broadcasting Authority (IBA), as the telecommunications regulator. The Act also established the Universal Service Agency (USA) as the primary mechanism for the provision of access throughout the country.

The main telecommunications operator is a former state-owned monopoly Telkom, which still has a monopoly on fixed lines. Telkom's exclusivity and the introduction of a second network operator were effected by the Telecommunications Amendment Act of 2001. The government has introduced special licenses to small, medium and micro enterprises to operate Public Switched Telephone networks (PSTN) in rural areas. There were 2.1 million fixed lines in 2001 and 9 million mobile subscribers (BMI-Technologies 2002: 403) in the country. The cellular phone share of the market has grown rapidly in the last few years, with three providers being Vodacom, MTN, and the newly established Cell C. There are currently more mobile than fixed lines in South Africa, a situation similar to that in Uganda, Senegal and most of the continent.

Other government departments and programmes also target ICTs, and several government initiatives are geared toward promoting ICTs. The Government Communications and Information Service, for example, has been involved in establishing 'Multi-Purpose Community Centres' for integrated government service delivery in disadvantaged areas and Schoolnet South Africa has projects in thousands of schools.

The USA has largely focussed on setting up ICT centres, generally called telecentres and cyberlabs in South Africa. Twelve of the telecentres set up by USA in South Africa have been with assistance from IDRC. At the end of 2001, USA had established 81 telecentres in different parts of the country.

The cost of establishing a telecentre in South Africa is said to be approximately ZAR 200,000 (USD 16,600). In most cases, the establishment process does not involve the construction of new buildings. The trend is to renovate existing buildings or shipping containers, make them secure, and paint them in the USA colours of white, purple, and green. Between one and four telephones are installed, and between two and five Pentium computers are set up. Most South African telecentres offer basic services such as telephone, photocopying, printing, and some word processing.

Study sites

The six telecentres that constituted the focus of this study are located in the Northern Province, which was chosen for several reasons:

- There were more USA telecentres in the Northern Province than in any other province in the country (a total of nine, four of which were jointly funded with IDRC);
- It is the province with the poorest telephone access and related services;
- Thabo Mbeki, the president of the Republic of South Africa, declared the province to be one of three that was to be a priority for development work;
- The University of the North has an Information Science Department that had declared its intention and interest in collaborating with the telecentre research; and
- The province is relatively close to Gauteng (the growing silicon valley of Africa), the offices of IDRC and USA, and Wits University, and this proximity facilitated the involvement of the principal stakeholders in the evaluation process.

USA selected the six study sites to ensure that both older and newer telecentres were included in the study. The older telecentres, established between 1998 and mid-1999 are: Botlokwa, Phalala, and Makuleke; whereas, the newer ones, established during 2000, are Mankweng, Bakgaga-ba-Mothapo, and Thakgalane. With the exception of the Mankweng telecentre, which is located in a township, all of the other telecentres selected for the study were either in rural (Phalala, Makuleke, and Thakgalane) or in semi-rural locations (Botlokwa and Bakgaga-ba-Mothapo).

- Thakgalane is a village established in 1975. The population is estimated to be 9,646 with about 1,290 families. Thakgalane is situated on 11,000 ha in the western part of Tzaneen, 90 km from Pietersburg and 18 km from the nearest town of Soekmekaar. A high level of unemployment characterizes it. Many people, retrenched from failing factories in East-Rand live in the area. The main source of income for the people is subsistence farming, which provides low incomes far below the poverty line. The government is the main employer of labour. Each family contributes ZAR 70 (about USD 6) for community development. The main languages spoken in the area are Northern Sotho and Xitsonga. The telecentre was established in late 1999 in the tribal office.

- Makuleke is predominantly Xitsonga speaking and is located in the former Gazankulu area near the Kruger National Park, approximately 80 km from Thohoyandau and 140 km west of Louis Trichardt. Makuleke is a relatively small village, with an estimated population of 19,000. About 60% of the population is unemployed and many migrate to Gauteng Province for work. There are generally no private telephone lines in the households and people rely on public telecommunication services offered by private service providers like Vodacom, MTN, and the telecentre. A small number of people have cellular phones. The nearest bank, shopping centre, and other facilities are 45 km away at Malamulele Township. The Makuleke telecentre was launched in August 1999.

- Bakgaga-ba-Mothapo is located in a predominantly Northern Sotho speaking community in Mothapo village, 40 km east of Pietersburg and 10 km from Mankweng. The total population is estimated to be 159,000. There are enormous problems with access to information and telecommunications. South Africa Telkom is in the process of installing automatic telephones in the village in an attempt to address this problem. A small number of villagers have cellular phones.

- Botlokwa is a semi-rural area on the northern motorway, located 56 km north of Pietersburg on the Louis Trichardt road. There are 10 villages in the area inhabited by about 65,000 people. The telecentre is located next to other public services such as the police station, post office, tribal authority offices, a community radio station, the constituency office, and Eskom Point, which supplied electricity to residents on a commercial basis. The Botlokwa telecentre was established in February 1999.

- Phalala, which comprises 42 villages, has a population of 333,615. Phalala borders Botswana and is about 150 km from Pietersburg and about 80 km from the nearest town of Ellisrus. Setswana and Sepedi are spoken in the area. Phalala has very high rates of unemployment and illiteracy. Transport, information, and communication services are inadequate. High school drop-out rates are high and poverty is increasing. Phalala was the site of the first USA telecentre, established in March 1998.

- Mankweng is a township 30 km east of Pietersburg, close to the University of the North (UNIN) and the provincial hospital. It is a middle-class settlement with many businesses and shopping centres. A fairly high level of literacy (80%), characterizes Mankweng Township and the majority of residents are either staff or students of the university. Telecommunication services are easily available in comparison with the other areas. The Mankweng Township telecentre was established by a group of women who were trained in micro-enterprise management following their group's successful application to USA. A hall in a learning centre was renovated, equipped and operations commenced in February 2000. The telecentre is in the same building as a learning centre, which attracts both children and adult learners, and has numerous other projects. However, because of the theft of equipment, by March 2000 the telecentre had ceased operations. At the time of the study, there were three computers and six telephone lines. Before the burglary, the centre had four computers, one 'five-in-one' printer with facsimile, telephone, photocopying, printing, and scanning capabilities. There was also a scanner, which was not working, and a photocopier. Outside the telecentre, many of the houses have telephone connections, and two computer-training centres were operating within the area. A local radio station operates from the University of the North (UNIN).

Findings

Of the six telecentres, three were not operational at the time of the study. At the Mankweng Telecentre, theft of equipment barely a month after it was launched in February 2000, had paralysed operations. At Thakgalane, neither the required equipment (including a working phone line) had been received nor proper training been given to the staff at the time of the study. The Makuleke telecentre had ceased operations on account of a large unpaid phone bill. Consequently, discussions that follow are based largely on information from the telecentres in Phalala, Bakgaga-ba-Mothapo, and Botlokwa, which were operational at the time of the investigations.

Equipment

The ICTs available at the telecentres at the time of the study included computers, printers, facsimile machines, telephones, scanners, television sets, and video cassette recorders.

Computers were the most common ICT equipment at the telecentres along with telephones, facsimile machines, and photocopiers. Botlokwa, with seven computers, had the highest number of computers, whereas the other telecentres each had four computers. With respect to telephones, Thakgalane was waiting to have six lines installed at the time of the study, Botlokwa had five lines, Bakgaga-ba-Mothapo had four lines, and Phalala had two lines. Telkom provided all telephone lines. Each telecentre had one photocopier and one facsimile machine.

Services offered

The equipment that was available at the telecentres reflected the services offered to community members. For example, in Botlokwa, photocopying was the service most frequently used by clients (49.1%) followed by telephone calls (28.3%), computer use (11.3%), and printing (9.4%). At Phalala, the pattern of use was different, with a majority of the clients making telephone calls (43.8%) and photocopying (14.6%); computer use and printing were not very popular, as only 6.3% of users requested each service. In Bakgaga, the telephone was most popular (47%), followed by photocopying (36%), facsimile service (9%), computer use (8%), and printing (4%). At Thakgalane, few services could be offered because of the absence of telephone lines. Some photocopying was done, and the available computers were not being used because of a software problem. The facsimile machine and printer at the centre were also not operational during the research period.

Purpose of use

The research revealed that the telecentre services were used for a variety of purposes: for social and health reasons (Botlokwa, Phalala, Bakgaga-ba-Mothapo), for education and training (Botlokwa and Phalala), for business and government information (Botlokwa and Bakgaga-ba-Mothapo), and for employment, computer training, project hosting, funeral services, and local news (Botlokwa). In Mankweng, before the burglary, the centre used to provide typing services for students (for assignments) and for the preparation of resumes. The centre also helped teachers to design school schedules and community members to design business cards, greetings cards, and programs for weddings, funerals, parties, ceremonies, and social gatherings. There was no Internet connection in Mankweng even before the burglary.

Phalala had developed a wider range of services than other telecentres. These services included a post office and a weekly home affairs service. Telecentre staff became more involved in providing information services because there had been no local newspaper or radio station. A team spearheaded by the telecentre staff had been organized to develop the first newspaper for the area.

User profiles

At the Bakgaga-ba-Mothapo and Phalala telecentres the majority of users were between 17 and 40 years of age (73.0% in Bakgaga-ba-Mothapo and 88.7% in Phalala). The under-16 and over-40 age groups were not frequent participants in the activities of the two telecentres. There was a significant difference in the age profile of the users in Botlokwa, where 48% of the users were 26–40 years old and 32% were over 40 years old. No data were gathered on users below 25 years of age.

Available gender data from the Botlokwa and Phalala telecentres did not reveal any consistent differences. At Botlokwa, gender disparity was minimal as 50.9% of the users were male and 49.1% were female. In Phalala, the gender gap was considerably wider with 42.2% male and 57.8% female. Although systematic data for Bakgaga-ba-Mothapo was not collected, the researchers observed that more females used the telephones.

Information about the occupations of the users of the telecentres in Botlokwa and Phalala presented interesting insights. In Botlokwa, over 30% of the users were from the education sub-sector, labourers (e.g., domestic workers and taxi-drivers etc.) constituted 20.5%, and the unemployed, and government officials, each constituted about 10% of users. In Phalala, the unemployed constituted the largest proportion of the users (35%), and educators came a distant second (18%) followed by students (14%). In Mankweng, teachers and members of the business community mostly used photocopying services, and the facsimile machine was popular with students who needed to send urgent application forms and materials.

Impediments to use

A wide range of factors that hindered access and use of telecentre facilities and services were identified:

- Cost was at the top of the list of perceived impediments. Many of those interviewed claimed that the cost of the services, especially telephony and facsimile transmission, was too high and should be reduced to make it competitive and affordable for the majority of potential users. This was particularly true where there were competing services in the area (e.g., Botlokwa, Mankweng, Makuleke, and Bakgaga-ba-Mothapo). Where there was little or no competition (e.g., Phalala), price was less of an issue.
- Many users mentioned infrastructure as an impediment. In Botlokwa, the size and quality of the premises was an issue. Other hindrances related to infrastructure included: the non-availability of electricity (Mankweng) or erratic power supply (Botlokwa and Phalala); the non-availability of telephone lines (Thakgalane); non-functional equipment (Mankweng, Thakalage, and Bakgaga-ba-Mothapo); and inadequate or insufficient equipment (Botlokwa). Only Phalala and Bakgaga had been connected to the Internet at the time of the evaluation.
- Security was raised as an issue at almost all telecentres. The Mankweng telecentre had already lost a computer and printers to burglars. Although there were still three computers remaining in Mankweng, it could not continue to offer printing services on account.
- Staffing problems were of two kinds – number and attitude. If there are too few staff (e.g., in Mankweng) they cannot cater to the needs of the clientele. The attitude of staff also has a major bearing on the success or failure of telecentres.
- Lack of publicity meant that: 'many people just know the telecentre but they do not know what it is and how it can assist them' (member of client organization, Phalala telecentre).
- Accessibility: Although the telecentre management at Mankweng had taken the initiative to put up a sign board at a nearby market to give directions to the telecentre, according to the researchers involved in the study, the directions provided were so confusing that: 'even some of the members of the Board of Directors who were familiar with the place seem to get lost because of the directions.' In addition to difficulty

with finding the location, distance was also seen to curtail access to services according to some respondents in Bakgaga-ba-Mothapo.
- A poor location (e.g., in Mankweng) meant that services were not reaching the most needy and disadvantaged groups. This telecentre was built in a location where most of the residents had access to a number of other facilities and communication channels.

Relevance

In general, various community groups contended that the telecentres help them to maintain contact and communications with family members and friends. The telecentres had also impacted on distances that had to be travelled in search of similar services located elsewhere.

Schools in Botlokwa heavily used the telephones, facsimile machines, photocopiers, and computers for word processing. Other organizations, however, felt that the telecentre in Botlokwa was being badly run. A member of the Youth Club said: 'this is the first opportunity for us to make inputs regarding the telecentre ... it has been run like a private company and is not serving the youth ...' Many other organizations voiced unhappiness with the way the telecentre was being run. A lack of consultation was reported, and it was perceived that the telecentre was enriching individuals rather than benefiting the community.

In Phalala, all those interviewed were overwhelmingly positive about the telecentre and saw it as a sign of progress and development in the area. A member of the burial society stated: 'as a community, we are impressed by the services the telecentre is offering.' The Mankweng community felt that the centre should develop new services, such as a community newsletter, become a local information centre, and initiate training in computers and other skills.

Ownership, management, and sustainability

The telecentres were 'owned' by various groups and associations, although it was not clear what ownership actually meant to the respondents because the USA had set up telecentres using a franchise model.

The Phalala telecentre was owned by a local civic organization, part of the South African National Civic Organization (SANCO), and was housed in a building donated by the council in the grounds of the sports stadium. The telecentre was run by a staff of three and made a profit of about ZAR 2,000

(USD 166) each month. The income was banked regularly and managed by SANCO. Some of the money was invested in equipment (a camera) so that the telecentre could offer that service thought to be highly profitable.

The community through the tribal authority, which had established a nine-member board to direct the activities of the telecentre, owned the Bakgaga-ba-Mothapo telecentre. The Thakgalane telecentre had a very competent and energetic manager, and was supported by the wider community.

The Makuleke telecentre was owned by the people of Makuleke and run by a manager and a group of volunteers. The six-member Board of Directors, which was charged with responsibility for ensuring the survival and sustainability of the telecentre, was reported to be weak and unresponsive to the problems of the telecentre.

The Mankweng telecentre was attached to a day-care centre and community library. It is owned and managed by the women's committee that ran the day-care centre. The telecentre was well managed, although because Mankweng had many telephones and computer training facilities, the telecentre had competition and the services were consequently not in great demand.

The Botlokwa Communications Awareness Forum owned the Botlokwa telecentre. The community was represented on an eight-member management committee, which met monthly to oversee the running of the centre and make decisions on day-to-day activities. The research indicated that there was on-going tension as some people felt the telecentre was being run for individual profit rather than as a development project.

During the provincial workshop that was held as part of the evaluation process to mark the end of the research cycle, suggestions were made of ways to guarantee the success and sustainability of the telecentres:

- Provide appropriate equipment in good working condition: Without equipment to deliver services, there is a lack of activity that quickly leads to frustration and loss of clientele.
- Ensure that there is local need for the services: Telecentres should be set up where there is a local need for the services they provide. If most people in an area already have access to telephones and computers (e.g., in Mankweng), the telecentre will suffer stiff competition. In such cases, the telecentre must create a niche for itself by providing other relevant services. It was suggested that to remain relevant telecentres should incorporate information provision and dissemination.

- Good managers and management: This may be the single largest determinant of success. The selection of a motivated manager who had 'entrepreneurial energy' and was trusted by the community, was critical. In addition, the manager had to have adequate training in the technical, financial, service, and management issues of running a telecentre. Poor management was guaranteed to end in telecentre failure (e.g., Makuleke). Good management practices were also suggested; for example, the telecentres should offer 24-hour services and remain open on weekends. This suggestion had the corollary that more staff would be needed.
- Community support: Telecentres that have integrated their work with existing community groups have been more successful (e.g., in Phalala, and less so in Botlokwa). Community support is also helpful for fund-raising and mobilization.
- Good marketing: For success, the telecentre must be well known and appreciated by people. This entails developing and maintaining links with community organizations, schools, and churches, and improving promotion by using all available means, including community radio and other media.
- Develop new services and remain innovative: The more successful telecentres had developed new services to meet the emerging needs of community members. Some examples included: the creation of a post office and home affairs office in Phalala; computer training in Phalala, Botlokwa, and Bakgaga-ba-Mothapo; the sale of stationery in Botlokwa; and collaboration with a local radio station in Botlokwa. Another suggestion was that computer literacy courses should be offered to community members at a minimal fee.
- Appropriate pricing: It was easier for local telecentre monopolies to make money (e.g., in Phalala), but when the telecentres were faced with competition, responsiveness and creative pricing were critical (e.g., in Bakgaga-ba-Mothapo). In contrast, in Makuleke, respondents felt that if lower prices had been charged for telephone services, the telecentre would have faired much better. Community telecentres have the added burden of competing with MTN and Vodacom public pay phones whose charges are very low.
- Security: The theft at the Mankweng telecentre demonstrated that it was important to take security measures to safeguard the equipment from theft or from destruction by other causes, such as fire.

Conclusion

The aim of the research was to collect information that would help local telecentre managers to improve the relevance and sustainability of their telecentres. It was also expected that a learning system would be developed to support self-assessment and evaluation. There were some signs that this was happening in Phalala and Bakgaga-ba-Mothapo. In both these telecentres, the research led to wider community involvement in management decisions and to greater community commitment to the telecentre. In Botlokwa, the research raised community tensions between the telecentre management and other organizations in the community. In Makuleke, the research revealed a real local need, and the dire consequences of incompetent management (in this case, the near collapse of the telecentre). In Thakgalane and Mankweng, the research highlighted problems that were not directly under the control of local actors, such as non-delivery of equipment and inappropriate choice of sites.

The results presented in this chapter suggest that although the establishment of a successful telecentre is not easy when there is local commitment, a clear and determined focus, and the necessary equipment and skills, sustainability and positive impacts can be found within the communities brought about by the telecentres. The success of Phalala community TC provides some support and preliminary evidence for the evolutionary thesis of telecentre development. As the first USA TC started in 1998, it can be said and seen to be in the user-fee independent phase.

Chapter 7
Telecentres in Senegal

Senegal is a Sahelian country situated at the extreme western tip of the African continent. It is bordered by Mauritania to the north, Mali to the east, and Guinea and Guinea Bissau to the south. Gambia, a sovereign country lies completely within Senegal to the south. With a population of 9.58 million in December 2000, Senegal has a population density of 35 people/km^2. Senegal's population is growing at an annual rate of 2.9% and 85% of its population is younger than 20 years. Women comprise about 51% of the total population, 58% of the people live in rural areas, Muslims make up 94% of the population, and there are several ethnic groups (Wolof, Sereer, Toucouleur, Peul, Diola, Mandingo, Balante, and Bassari).

Economic growth is sustained by the secondary and tertiary sectors. The primary sector, dominated by agriculture, accounted for 17.8% of GDP in 1998. The principal products include groundnuts, fish products, and phosphate. The transport and telecommunication sectors contributed 62% to GDP in 1998.

The national literacy rate (82% for women and 63% for men) is very high among individuals over 15 years of age. The cumulative percentage of children in full-time education (pre-school and primary) is about 84.2%. There are 5,793 general and vocational education schools with a total student population of 1,393,730.

Telecommunications context

A semi-autonomous telecommunications regulatory body ART (Agence de Régulation des Télécommunications) was established late in 2001 despite provisions for it having been made in the Telecommunications Law of 1996. The telecommunications sector is dominated by SONATEL (Société Nationale des Télécommunications du Sénégal), a public service provider privatized in 1997 and partly owned by France Telecom. Created in 1985 after the split in the posts and telecommunication agency, TéléSénéga, SONATEL has a monopoly for fixed telephony, telex, telegraphy, access to international operators and switched packet data transmission up to 2006. SONATEL is the only national fixed operator and it also provides mobile services. SONATEL's mobile operator (Alizé) that was joined by SENTEL in the provision of GSM services in 1999 has exclusivity until 2004 and had an estimated 273,000 subscribers in 2001. SENTEL had a subscriber base of over 100,000 in the same period.

The Senegal telecommunications system has these characteristics:

- All thirty divisions of the country are connected to the general network by a digital transmission link, which ensures that the transmission network is fully digital (ISDN). Twenty-two out of the thirty divisions are linked to the general network by an optical fibre transmission link;
- A digital GSM cellular network, implemented by SONATEL, covers the major towns and roads of the country and is interconnected with foreign networks (Spain, Great Britain, and Italy);
- 2,000 km of optical fibres encircle the country and are the property of SONATEL;
- SONATEL is the main source of international bandwidth (i.e., gateway) Senegal has a 64 bps link with the USA via MCI. SONATEL has a 45 Mbps link to France and a 3 Mbps link to Teleglobe in Canada, with a 4 Mbps link to The Gambia;
- SONATEL's telecommunications infrastructure changed dramatically in 2002 with the launch of Atlantis-2 and SAT-3/WASC cables that land in Dakar and connect the country directly to most other coastal African countries, Latin America, Europe and Asia via multi gigabit optic fibre links, which will be expanded via terrestrial fibre to Mali and Mauritania.
- There are 15 Internet Service Providers (ISP) in the country, most of them are in Dakar and a few in Saint Louis; e.g., Metissacana, Arc Informatique, Point Net, University of Saint-Louis, Primature, ORSTOM, AfricaOnline, etc.
- The total number of telephone lines increased from 81,000 lines in 1998 to over 223, 474 in June. Close to 70% of the telephone lines are

to be found in Dakar. In July, 2001, there were a total of 360,000 mobile subscribers in the country; and

All rural communities have fixed-lines telephone access and many of them now have access to the mobile phones, especially those areas located along the main roads.

In September 2000, SONATEL reported that there were 8,200 telecentres active in Senegal. The last census conducted by SONATEL in 1999, identified 20 cybercafés and 80 telecentres connected to the Internet nation-wide. With improved bandwidth of up to 42 Mbps announced by SONATEL (*Sud Quotidien*, 26 December 2000), an increase in the use of the Internet is expected. Telecentres in Senegal vary greatly in size, from one room, one-telephone shops to large cybercafés holding a range of equipment. Although all are called telecentres, the majority of them would more rightly be described as telephone kiosks or phone shops following the typography proposed by Gomez et al. (1999:15).

The telecommunications sector has witnessed significant changes, which have begun to pay dividends. In the 1980s, average annual investments in the sector exceeded FCFA 18 billion. In 1996, the telecom sector directly contributed to an increase in the GDP of 2.6%. In addition, it acted as a driving force for other national economic activities. About 10,000 jobs were created by the sector between 1992 and 1998.

Despite the impressive statistics, telecommunication costs remain high and services are not accessible to all because of the level of infrastructure development in the rural areas and poverty, which makes it difficult for some sections of the population to pay for services. Connection tariffs vary between FCFA 9,600 and 15,000 for a telephone line and the cost of a local telephone call is a standard FCFA 60 (per unit of 2 minutes) USD 0.08 and a national call costs about the same for 1 minute. Senegal has a policy of lower telephone charges to the Internet and international calls.

Twenty telecentres were investigated in Senegal. Data was collected between November 2000 and February 2001 using five types of data collection instruments: observation; discussion and document analysis guides; interview schedules; and individual and organizational questionnaires. The sample consisted of 1,019 survey respondents, 220 users, 27 organizational leaders, 13 telecentre managers, 14 community leaders, 5 telecom officials, and 4 staff of local authorities. Focus group discussions were conducted with management committee members, youth, and women.

Context of telecentres

The 20 telecentres in the study are located in the central and northern regions of Senegal. The telecentres fall under three institutional arrangements: those administered by Enda and referred to as Enda-Ecopop telecentres, which are part of an ICT project started in 1998; those run by Trade Point Senegal (TPS) an UNCTAD project started in 1999 for which IDRC is a partner; and private telecentres.

ENDA-ECOPOP Telecentres

Enda-Ecopop implements activities in the disadvantaged urban and peri-urban areas and neighbourhoods of Dakar, where it provides technical and institutional support to the telecentres. Each telecentre is associated with a community resource centre (CRC) run by a management committee. The CRCs bring together a network of non-professional organizations in the neighbourhoods surrounding the centre. Four of the eight telecentres investigated are located in the central neighbourhoods of Félix Eboué, Médina, Sicap, and Colobane. These are islands of poverty amid the plenty so visible in other parts of the downtown area. The other telecentres are in the outskirts of Dakar in Pikine and Yeumbeul, and further away in Rufisque and Yarakh.

Enda-Ecopop is involved in the implementation of integrated activities in health, education, sanitation, micro-projects, and micro-financing in the communities in which their projects are located. The Acacia Initiative had a working partnership with Enda-Ecopop in Senegal for the telecentres project.

TPS Telecentres

Trade Point Senegal (TPS) provides technical and administrative support to a number of regional telecentre sites. The local municipality or chamber of commerce hosts each TPS telecentre. The hosts are represented on the management committees of the telecentres as local principal partners. The TPS telecentres are located in Guédiawaye, Mboro, Joal, and Saint Louis, all of which are heterogeneous sociocultural environments.

Guédiawaye is a suburban neighbourhood on the outskirts of Dakar characterized by a high population, high levels of poverty, poor infrastructure, a very high level of illiteracy, and a thriving informal sector. Mboro in Thiès has highly developed infrastructure because it is situated near the foremost mining industry in the country (Chemical Industries of Senegal). The telecentre in Joal is located in a new migrant fishing neighbourhood. The main economic and, to a certain extent, social activities are related to fishing. In Saint-Louis, one of Senegal's older towns, the telecentre is located in the town's Chamber of Commerce, Industry and Local Crafts, which is situated in the administrative part of the town. This confers a degree of formality on the telecentre, which in turn affects community dynamics around the telecentre.

Findings

Telecentre physical facilities

The telecentres were generally not located in premises originally built for this use. They are usually found in premises that belonged to local communities, associations, or chambers of commerce, such as in Mboro, Saint Louis, Yarakh, Pikine, and Yeumbeul, or in rented premises that had initially been designed for other types of use such as in Joal.

The telecentres look very cramped because most premises are narrow and not very comfortable. However, some managers had successfully arranged the interiors in such a way as to make space for waiting room areas with chairs and ensuring ventilation. Two telecentres, Saint Louis and Joal, had air-conditioning.

Most telecentres did not guarantee privacy. The telephones and computers were usually in the room that also served as the waiting room. Very few telecentres made reading materials (e.g., journals and magazines) available to waiting customers, and very few had their own toilets for the exclusive use of the telecentre and its users. The quality of the furniture and equipment varied from one telecentre to the next but was generally good. However, the computer hardware was less impressive in terms of quality and quantity. Users often spent a lot of time trying to obtain connections or perform simple tasks.

In general, the space occupied by the telecentres was inadequate and usually did not conform to SONATEL's standard requirement of 12 m^2. The space limitations did not allow the telecentres to provide users and staff with ideal services and comfortable environments for reception areas or workspaces. Most of the telecentres did not engender privacy and about one quarter of the ones in the study sample occupied a single room.

Services offered

The telecentres offer a range of services: telephone, Internet access, email, web-page design, word processing, and training. In addition to these services offered by community telecentres, some private telecentres have developed other services and products not directly related to ICTs such as the sale of cosmetics, beverages and a number of other commodities. Specific products and services offered by the various telecentres included:

- Production of business vouchers, invoices, delivery notes, posters, letterheads with logos, and business, invitation, and greetings cards;
- Dispatch and receipt of messages;
- Search for partners (local and distant) and markets for local products;
- Creation of email addresses and accounts;
- Access to information about world trade fairs (e.g., dates, venues, and conditions of attendance)
- Provision of guidance and searches for opportunities for pupils and students wishing to pursue studies overseas (Foreign Students Assistance);
- Production of promotional materials (e.g., posters and product labels for processed and unprocessed products); and
- Training and tools for financial management, hygiene, dyeing, and the processing of local products.

Each type of telecentre offered specific services, sometimes depending on its location. For example, in the TPS sites, the telecentres translated information about business opportunities that was disseminated by the UNCTAD global network to which TPS is affiliated. No such specialized services were being provided in the Enda-Ecopop sites; whereas the private telecentres provided facsimile services, which the others did not usually provide.

In the Enda-Ecopop telecentres, as in most others, the telephone was most popular, but in both the private telecentres and the TPS telecentres, the Internet and, in particular, email was very popular. Some private telecentres had video libraries in addition to other commercial services. Although the private telecentres were clearly profit-oriented, the activities in the Enda-Ecopop sites were community related and provided support for savings and credit, community management of water and electricity, advice to neighbourhood organizations about maintaining electronic files of members, financial management, and the management of electronic databases.

Use

Telecentres in Senegal are a recent discovery. They were first set up in 1992 and the twelve Acacia telecentres in the survey sample date back to 1998. The uses to which telecentres are put are many and varied. At the time of the study in 2000–2001 only 5% of users had been using telecentres for more than 2 years and 65% of those interviewed had used them for less than 1 year.

Table 27. Length of telecentre use

	ACACIA TCs		Control TCs		Total
3 months	21	(75.0%)	7	(25.0%)	28
6 months	18	(81.8%)	4	(18.2%)	22
Less than 1 year	43	(67.2%)	21	(32.8%)	64
1 to 2 years	51	(77.3%)	15	(22.7%)	66
2 to 5 years	7	(43.8%)	9	(56.3%)	16
5 years and +	2	(40.0%)	3	(60.0%)	5
Not declared			1	(100.0%)	1
Total	170	(70.5%)	71	(29.5%)	241

Telephony was the most popular service at most of the telecentres. In the Enda-Ecopop and private telecentres, the telephone was the most heavily used service. Its extensive use has turned the telephone into a very ordinary yet powerful tool.

The Enda-Ecopop telecentres were also used as meeting places in the difficult and harsh socioeconomic environment of the city. They provided sites that helped maintain linkages between the urban community and communities of origin, which were scattered all over the country. The telephones were being used as collective community answering machines, almost free for community members who could not afford the cost. In Baraka, for example, the community had installed a line dedicated to incoming calls at its own expense. This service has been hugely beneficial to some groups. Female domestic workers from disadvantaged neighbourhoods were in the habit of clustering in street corners usually under the elements (the intense sun, heavy dust, and occasional rain showers) as they waited to be hired by affluent city residents. They were often exposed to real risks and found this service to be tremendously useful. The Enda-Ecopop project made the use of telephones for advertising a reality for this group. The women used the telecentres to advertise their skills and availability. This provided them safer means for their job searches. However, users felt that the telephone services in the Enda-Ecopop telecentres were inadequate, possibly because of their popularity and the pressure on their use.

Before the introduction of these projects the personal computer was almost unknown in most of the project sites and the majority of respondents discovered computers at the telecentres. Project computers were most frequently used for office tasks, to capture or store data by business people and small groups (e.g., artisans and other micro-enterprises), and for record keeping by community associations.

Internet use was low in many telecentres with the exception of the TPS ones. Even when used, the telecentre staff usually did all the surfing for customers. Only a handful of students used the Internet themselves to search for registration information for foreign universities. It was very rare to find lay people accessing the Internet by themselves. Specialized services related to trade were offered by the TPS for tradesmen who were looking for business opportunities. This service was not available in the Enda Community Resource Centres/telecentres. Tradespeople from towns such as Thiés and Saint-Louis and remote rural areas like Ross Béthio and Podor were using this service from TPS telecentres. The Serbatim TPS telecentre had developed an extensive and interesting partnership network through which it had found and nurtured many business opportunities.

Table 28. Sex of users

Gender	ACACIA TCs	Control TCs	Total	% in relation to total
Female	34 (61.8%)	21 (38.2%)	55	23%
Male	136 (73.1%)	50 (26.9%)	186	77%
Total	170 (70.5%)	71 (29.5%)	241	100%

Source: Survey, November 2000.

Table 29. Age of users

Age	ACACIA TCs	Control TCs	Total	% in relation to total
Under 19 years	10 (71.4%)	4 (28.6%)	14	6%
19 to 30 years	81 (68.6%)	37 (31.4%)	118	50%
31 to 45 years	50 (72.5%)	19 (27.5%)	69	29%
46 to 55 years	18 (72.0%)	7 (28.0%)	25	11%
56 and over	6 7(5.0%)	2 (25.0%)	8	3%
Total	165 (70.5%)	69 (29.5%)	234	100%

Source: Survey, November 2000.

The telecentres allow users to perform a significant social function – maintaining social and business contacts in Senegal and around the world. Of the householders who were interviewed, 88% maintained contact with persons residing in Dakar, 79% maintained contact with persons in other parts of Senegal; and 24% maintained contact with individuals in other parts of Africa while 45% maintained contact with people in other parts of the world (Table 31). It is interesting to note that nearly twice the number of people maintain contacts with the rest of the world as with Africa.

User profiles

The majority of the telecentre users were men. They represented 80% of the users in the Enda-Ecopop telecentres and 70% in the others. However, only 51.3% of the men in the random survey sample claimed to use the telecentres. The largest group of users (90%) were between 19 and 55 years of age. The survey results show that all age groups used the telecentres, but youth and adults between the ages of 30 and 55 years were by far the most frequent users, possibly because they were the most economically and socially active.

The telecentres were also used by organizations. Interviews with organizational representatives revealed that the telecentres were used quite heavily. Six of the eleven organizations relied on the telecentres as their main source of information, the nature of which ranged from health, to sports, and trading.

Beneficiaries

Other than direct users, a large number of individuals qualify as beneficiaries of the services provided by the telecentres because of extensive and pervasive social occupational, family, religious, and political networks typical in Senegal. All the members of the local community were considered to be beneficiaries of the telecentres, but the main beneficiaries were members of the user's household, parents, in-laws, friends with whom obtained information is shared, business and social acquaintances, association members for whom the user acted as a representative, and local communities and businesses, for whom the centre acts as advisor.

The in-depth case study found 29 users who had conveyed the information they had received from the telecentres to 62 other people: friends (13), spouses (10), colleagues (8), and cousins (6). The information was first shared with family members (30), then with their network of friends (13), and ultimately with work colleagues (9). The survey results show that all social groups derived secondary benefit from the telecentre services. This suggests that the telecentre can be a powerful tool for driving social change if information collected can be spread to twice the number of physical visitors to the telecentre.

Table 30. Contacts maintained through the telecentres with others in Dakar, Senegal, Africa, the rest of the world

	Dakar		Senegal		Africa		World	
	Yes (%)	No (%)	Yes (%)	No (%)	Yes (%)	No (%)	Yes (%)	No (%)
Yarakh	75 (89)	9 (11)	68 (81)	16 (19)	18 (22)	65 (78)	34 (42)	48 (59)
Joal	76 (75)	25 (25)	75 (77)	22 (23)	21 (25)	62 (75)	34 (39)	53 (61)
Mboro	67 (68)	32 (32)	70 (71)	29 (29)	15 (15)	84 (85)	33 (33)	66 (67)
Pikine	97 (97)	3 (3)	83 (83)	17 (17)	21 (21)	79 (79)	50 (50)	50 (50)
Rufisque	99 (99)	1 (1)	83 (83)	17 (17)	19 (19)	80 (81)	48 (48)	52 (52)
Saint Louis	67 (91)	7 (10)	55 (76)	17 (24)	19 (38)	31 (81)	43 (66)	22 (34)
Rail	53 (95)	3 (5)	39 (72)	15 (28)	12 (24)	39 (77)	17 (34)	33 (66)
Colobane	68 (100)	—	64 (96)	3 (5)	10 (17)	49 (83)	29 (44)	37 (56)
Baraka	66 (87)	10 (13)	57 (79)	15 (21)	28 (50)	28 (50)	15 (31)	34 (69)
Médina	68 (100)	—	63 (93)	5 (7)	19 (34)	37 (66)	34 (57)	26 (43)
Guédiawaye	58 (69)	26 (31)	34 (42)	47 (58)	7 (11)	56 (89)	30 (40)	46 (61)
Yeumbeul	100 (99)	1 (1)	98 (97)	3 (3)	28 (28)	73 (72)	55 (55)	45 (45)
Total	894 (88)	117 (12)	789 (79)	206 (21)	217 (24)	683 (76)	422 (45)	512 (55)

Source: Survey November 2000.

Quality of service

The majority of users (78%) stated that the services offered by both the private and community telecentres were adequate, and more than 80% claimed to be satisfied with the information they obtained from the telecentres.

The major success factors associated with the community telecentres were identified as socioeconomic and cultural. The community resource centres (CRCs, Enda-Ecopop) served as economic, social, and cultural centres where people living in disadvantaged neighbourhoods or rural areas had access to ICTs because of the proximity of the centres and the affordability of tariffs. The CRC telecentre managers were also in the habit of providing advice and assistance to users. The majority of users indicated that they would love to see some improvements in the physical facilities and premises of the telecentres.

Although the use of telecentres has become very popular in Senegal, some groups have been marginalized. The groups with the greatest difficulties are the poor and disadvantaged (students, the unemployed, and women). It was reported that illiteracy did not appear to be a major constraint to access and use of the telecentres because of the assistance provided by telecentre managers and the language used to transact business that was the local one. More than 80% of the community members who were interviewed expressed satisfaction indicating that their information needs had been met by the community telecentres.

Common problems

Service delivery in the telecentres was affected by common technical and infrastructure problems. The most severe problems were computer failures, printer breakdowns, and corrupted software. Routine computer maintenance disrupted services and greatly displeased users. This was because for the majority of the telecentres in the study this involved physically moving the systems to Dakar for the required maintenance. The process took long. On the other hand, bringing technicians from Dakar also meant appreciable disruptions to use timetables since the way to justify this line of action would be a major breakdown. Second in degree of importance were electrical/ electricity problems, principally power failures or interruptions. Telephone and connection problems were commonly manifest as busy dial tones and signal loss by which users were not terribly bothered, as they had got used to this irritation. The cost of use did not surface as a serious impediment, except among disadvantaged groups, such as the unemployed, students, and women.

Staff members in all the telecentres lacked the skills and expertise needed to solve identified problems by themselves. Technical problems encountered by the community resource centres were referred to the main resource centre, which was located in Dakar's Blaise Senghor Cultural Centre and served as the hub for all the community resource centres and was the central repair node for the Enda-Ecopop project. The TPS technical department was responsible for solving problems in the TPS telecentres.

Relevance

The services provided at the telecentres were described as useful and relevant because they were serving the social and economic needs of the people and were requested by all the different groups in the community: farmers, artisans, business people, women's groups, sports and cultural associations, and students. The information about business opportunities was said to have helped improve and develop business activities by adding value to products and services. The facilitation of access to distant markets and products had contributed to improvements in community organizations. The local production of illustrated brochures with the use of scanners, business invoices, members' lists, dues, checklists, and minutes were all cited as examples of content-development activities.

The use of email in place of telegrams, which require lots of time to process and many hours to deliver, also improved businesses. The use of email by Senegalese migrant workers in other parts of the world and to effect money transfers was a case in point. It was unclear from the research report how this was accomplished but other sources suggest that through email messages, money would be made available to say a family member located in Dakar by an individual in Senegal. The refund is made to such an individual's kin or contact located in an address overseas usually Europe or America. All the messaging and necessary confirmations and contacts are made possible by email.

Although the services provided by the telecentres were considered to be very relevant and appropriate for the needs of the population, the picture with content and applications was different. Efforts were being made by the telecentres to address issues in the local environment and the community telecentres were designed around themes that reflected the daily concerns of the local people for which content and applications were being sought with little success. In Saint-Louis and Joal the search for markets for fish was a daily concern for a large part of the population. In Mboro, people looked to sell their market-garden produce, and in Guédiawaye, sculptures and dyed articles had to find a market. The concern in Baraka was for education and alternative training, in Rail, residents were concerned with crafts, and in Yeumbeul, community health was a key concern. The telecentre in Rufisque was grappling with sanitation and housing issues, Yarakh, with childhood and youth problems, and in Colobane with women and local development problems. In Pikine, the telecentre was attempting to develop savings and credit strategies for women, and in Médina, support for associations and cultural activities were the main issues of concern for applications development.

Despite this expressed concern for thematic information needs, the development of content and applications had not progressed very well because of the dearth of requisite skills among telecentre staff and the absence of sophistication in the communities themselves. Although the requisite expertise was absent, the telecentre staff maintained constant dialogue with the local communities and some really elementary and generic products and services were designed and developed to respond to some of the community needs. The most advanced products designed were logos, letterheads, business cards, invitation cards, job certificates, posters for popular entertainment events, and these were made by simple use of word processing and graphics software packages. These products were usually designed after project staff had analyzed the needs and the environment using participatory approaches with local community members.

The level of content and the applications that had been created at the time of the study were not very sophisticated and it could be argued that they were not applications in the true sense of the word. Therefore the road to real (genuine) content development of relevant and useable applications is still long.

Ownership, management, and sustainability

The ownership frameworks in the Enda-Ecopop and TPS telecentres were not the same. Each of the telecentres had different partners, and the dynamics in the surrounding communities were unique and specific. The Enda-Ecopop telecentres were commonly seen as owned by the communities, whereas the TPS sites were described as belonging to individuals or associations. Unlike private telecentres, the TPS and Enda-Ecopop telecentres were conceptualized as having close community involvement through community organizations that were primary stakeholders who provided support to the projects. Local partners often provided the telecentres with much needed additional capital. This community support energized the telecentre activities, assisted their development, and contributed to their sustainability.

However, the various actors understood the notion of ownership differently. Residents perceived the community telecentres, which were started in partnership with Enda-Ecopop, as belonging to the community. The communities were deeply involved in their management and the telecentres were fairly well integrated into the environment and had been accepted by the people. The telecentres operated in partnership with TPS were considered as belonging to private companies that were merely providing services to the community. Respondents averred that for a telecentre to be sustainable the community had to be the rightful owner and that this could be achieved through community-based organizations. Most, if not all, of the telecentres investigated were being run as pilot projects with the intermediate institutions acting as parents. This situation is quite unlike the private telecentres.

Community participation in management

Both the TPS and Enda-Ecopop telecentres had management committees made up of representatives of local communities, local chambers of commerce, and business people. The number of members varied from one telecentre to the other. In Enda-Ecopop, there were as many men as women. There were also representatives from other significant interest groups, such as community-based organizations located in the surrounding neighbourhoods, in the Enda-Ecopop telecentres.

The communities expressed satisfaction with the management and based this judgement on the availability and skills of the telecentre staff. However, they noted that no information on the technical and financial management of the telecentre was made available to community members. Several other observations were made about telecentre management. The administrative, financial, and technical management of the TPS telecentres was centralized in the head office in Dakar, where all the important decisions relating to the running of the telecentres were taken. The manager was unable to authorize or incur any type of expense, not even for the procurement of computer supplies or stationery. In the event of technical problems, managers were usually unable to solve these problems even when they were minor faults such as computer or printer breakdowns. All problems had to be referred to the head office, and this usually entailed waiting for technicians to arrive from Dakar or for the faulty equipment to be physically moved to Dakar. No maintenance contracts had been signed with local technicians to provide services, and relying on Dakar resulted in service interruptions for several days at the telecentres. This, 'distance management' engaged in by the head office negatively affected the TPS telecentres.

The managers in the Enda-Ecopop telecentres reported having simple reporting tools. A management system jointly developed between the telecentre staff and the management committee was used. The managers were in charge of running expenses such as bills (e.g., telecom, electricity, rent, management, and savings), and the surplus was placed in a reserve account and used according to the discretion of the management committees. In the TPS telecentres, unlike the Enda-Ecopop telecentres, the management committees did not feel like owners because they were neither involved in the financial and technical management nor in the recruitment of staff and were not involved in awareness-raising activities on behalf of the telecentres.

The Guédiawaye telecentre was seen as a model of true ownership and good management practices that ensured genuine community involvement and reaped sustainability on account of its management and entrepreneurial model. This telecentre is owned by a group of 1,200 (mostly women) members and managed by an appointed management committee that reports regularly to the members. All staff members come from the community, and there is collective responsibility for running the telecentre and for ensuring its sustainability by creative marketing and other non-ICT products.

These findings suggest that the issues of telecentre ownership, management and sustainability ought to be de-linked or at the minimum problematised more sensitively. Three types of ownership patterns were evident – private individual/s, private group or company (e.g., Guédiawaye) and quasi community ownership better seen as a trusteeship. None of these ownership variations was found to be consistently associated with a particular management outcome, although private telecentres did tend to make more profits. The least developed model – that of trusteeship – was the most common form of ownership in the Enda-Ecopop telecentres and in some of the TPS ones. It requires to be better understood by both designers and implementers if success is to be achieved.

Finances

The financial picture discussed in this section is based on the financial summary of the Enda-Ecopop telecentres from August 2000 to January 2001 and financial statements from the TPS evaluation report. The financial situation of some private telecentres was used for comparison. Table 31 provides a profile of expenditures and costs in some of the telecentres.

Income

In the Enda-Ecopop telecentres, telephony was the main source of income and accounted for more than 80% of revenue. In comparison, other services such as word processing and training generated about 13% of total income. Income from telephony was practically nonexistent in the TPS telecentres, where most revenue came from Internet access (41.0%), web products (17.8%), and 'other sources' (20.0%).

Sundry non-ICT income represented a noticeable percentage for private telecentres whose ICT services generated small revenues comprising 7.6% of total income. Monthly revenues ranged from about FCFA 1.5 million in the Enda-Ecopop telecentres, to less than FCFA 5,000 in the TPS telecentres, to hundreds of thousands of FCFA in the private facilities (Exchange rate: USD1=FCFA 740). The total income of the Enda-Ecopop telecentres was more than double that of the TPS telecentres. There were also large variations in income generation between the different telecentres of the same project (Enda-Ecopop or TPS). Among the Enda-Ecopop telecentres, Yeumbeul earned on average over FCFA 500,000 (676.00 USD) each month; whereas, Yarakh earned about FCFA 20,000 (27 USD). The differences among the TPS telecentres were even greater, with amounts varying from a few thousand to over a hundred thousand FCFA. This finding is further evidence that ownership patterns alone do not confer sustainability.

Table 31. Monthly incomes and expenditures at three types of telecentres in Senegal

	Telephone	Internet	Office automation	Training	Infocom	Web products	Other*	Personnel	Total
Income									
Enda-Ecopop	1,285,797 86.7%	24,774 1.7%	130,537 8.8%	49,167 3.3%	0 —	0 —	0 —	0 —	1,483,749
TPS	2,714 0.4%	251,093 41.0%	31,394 5.1%	0 —	95,202 15.6%	108,979 17.8%	122,842 20.1%	0 —	612,223
Private	343,125 68.3%	38,125 7.6%	0 —	0 —	0 —	0 —	121,442 24.2%	0 —	502,692
Expenditures									
Enda-Ecopop	1,065,565 77.6%	48,667 3.6%	48,997 3.6%	10,000 0.7%	0 —	0 —	66,597 4.9%	132,593 9.7%	1,372,419
TPS	494,440 20.7%	0 —	132,000 5.5%	0 —	0 —	0 —	82,250 3.4%	1,680,000 70.3%	2,388,69
Private	278,699 62.4%	0 —	0 —	0 —	0 —	0 —	127,975 28.7%	40,000 9.0%	446,675

Source: Survey February 2001.
* Includes the sale of such items as soft drinks and other products.

Expenditure

Whereas the Enda-Ecopop telecentres spent about 92% of their generated incomes, the TPS sites spent nearly four times (390%) more than their revenues (Table 31 and Figure 8). The private telecentres spent on average less than either of the other two. Telephone expenditures were highest for all telecentres. It is curious that even in the TPS telecentres, a sizeable amount was spent on telephones, which did not fetch an equivalent amount in revenue, yet practically nothing was spent on web products, which generated most of the money.

Telephone (connectivity) costs constituted the second largest expenditure item (Table 31) after salaries. Expenditure on staff in the Enda-Ecopop and private telecentres accounted for 10% of total expenses, but 70% in the TPS telecentres. Other expenditures, including electricity, stationery, computer supplies, and, less frequently, housing, accounted for 10–12% of total expenditures. The community (Enda-Ecopop and TPS) telecentres often did not pay rent. A rank ordering shows that salaries come at the top in a scale of expenditure followed by telephone and computer supplies.

Sustainability

The findings suggest that telecentres have the potential for sustainability on account of their social and economic utility and their capacity to respond to the ICT needs of the population. Services provided by the telecentres were greatly appreciated by community members. Some of the telecentres especially the Enda-Ecopop ones that were located in disadvantaged neighbourhoods had become popular meeting places for community members and organizations. The telecentres had become a vital and integral part of the community's social infrastructure. The report argues that telecentre sustainability depends on their successful integration into the community, their acceptance by the people, and the enthusiasm of the community to get involved in their management. It is therefore possible on the basis of this argument to distinguish institutional sustainability from conceptual validity on one hand and financial sustainability on the other. It does seem that conceptual validity and institutional validity are logically linked to the extent that an idea has found acceptance, value and concrete expression among the population. The concept is recreated and encapsulated in the institution of the telecentre. The existence and validity of the idea is therefore guaranteed but the nature and form of future mutations of the institutions and indeed the idea may not necessarily follow those of the initial conception. The point was repeatedly made that conceptual validity confers on the telecentre institutional sustainability.

Financial sustainability for community telecentres remains elusive. Given the amount of revenues generated by the telecentres, with which few could cover their total running expenses, this conclusion cannot be avoided. Despite steadily increasing incomes, 50–70% of income was being spent on salaries. This situation does not generate financial confidence, stability, or sustainability. The funds provided by IDRC and other donors have assured that the telecentres will survive for as long as the projects last. However, because all projects eventually end, it is important that telecentres develop strategies for self-sufficiency by generating income and raising funds from local partners such as chambers of commerce. The Acacia program is currently considering different models for the future of those telecentres in which it is involved. These futures exclude the continuation of full support, which makes the issue of sustainability a priority. Short-term resources in the form of working capital, combined with guarantees of resources in the medium and long term, are needed to ensure the sustainability of the telecentres.

The Guédiawaye community telecentre is one success. Owned and run by a community based-organization – the SERBATIM Economic Interest Group (EIG), the telecentre has shown that community TCs can generate enough revenue to cover their operating costs and make profit. The SERBATIM EIG has 1,200 members (957 women and 243 men) and was incorporated in 1997 to implement income-generating activities for the benefit of its members. At the time of the study, it was carrying out various activities, which ranged from dyeing, to the production of wooden sculptures and other works of art, to computer training. The group owned a hairdressing salon to provide training for youth, a savings and credit facility, a day-care nursery, and a private school. These profit-making activities, together with members' dues, were generating sufficient financial resources to cover all expenses. The telecentre staff and members of the EIG, had worked for almost a year on a voluntary basis and began to receive monthly allowances only when the group became financially stable. The telecentre was running without any major external subsidies, except for the fact that like most other telecentres, the premises were free. Here, therefore, is an example of a

Volume 2: The Experience with Community Telecentres

Figure 7. Telecentre income in FCFA

Legend: Personnel, Other*, Web Products, Infocom, Training, Office, Internet, Telephone

Telecentre: Enda-Eco, TPS, Private

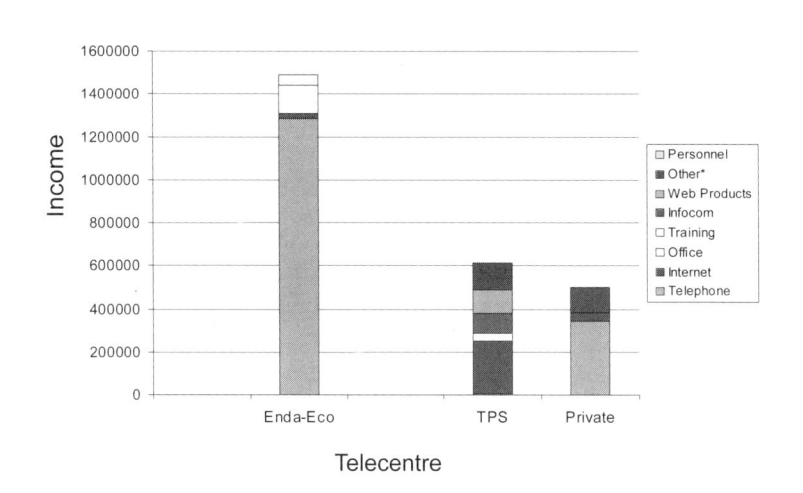

Figure 8. Telecentre expenditure in FCFA

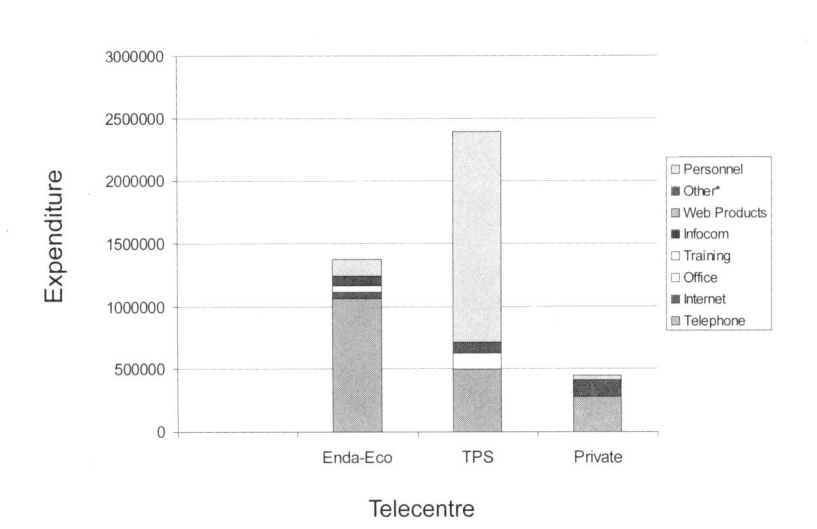

Legend: Personnel, Other*, Web Products, Infocom, Training, Office, Internet, Telephone

Telecentre: Enda-Eco, TPS, Private

147

community TC run on an entrepreneurial model designed to benefit members. Technically speaking the motive of the CBO is profit making and a variety of products were created to ensure that sufficient revenue was generated to satisfy members. Members were also willing to volunteer services until such a time, as the investment was ripe. Clearly there is a real need to study this model more closely.

Other community TCs whose core motives were perhaps less identifiable with profit and enrichment were not concerned by their lack of profitability, preferring instead to dwell on the fact of their proven institutional sustainability in the belief that they were providing services that were of great value to the community. Therefore, their continued existence could be justified on the basis that they are a public good.

Summary and conclusion

This study has shown that:

- Communities use telecentre services in their daily lives to satisfy their social and economic needs, such as to send and receive messages and seek information.
- Communities are satisfied both with the community telecentres and the services they offer.
- The social impact of the telecentres is significant.
- The introduction and development of the telephone, especially with the advent of the telecentres, has given birth to a new telephone culture. People are now conscious of the telephone as a means of both social and business communication, and this has reduced reliance on the transportation system as virtual mobility has become a reality.
- The new technologies provide access without social discrimination or marginalization.
- The telecentre is at one and the same time an ICT service provider, a forum for training, a centre for hosting neighbourhood micro-enterprises and individual entrepreneurs, and a shared secretariat.
- The telecentres have enhanced local job opportunities and the acquisition of new skills.
- Some telecentres have contributed to the strengthening of community organizations and the linkages between them. Telecentres now play a

- supportive and advisory role and act as intermediaries in the information and communication chain in the community.
- Some telecentres have influenced the financial behaviour of community members by establishing local savings and credit schemes.
- A central research task for the study was to determine which management model might be best from the perspective of sustainability. Difficult as it was to compare between the models because they had different products and strengths, it is clear that the relationship between ownership, management and sustainability is complex and in need of further study. The community-oriented model represented by the Enda-Ecopop telecentres facilitated access and social integration of underprivileged people. The quasi business model exemplified by the TPS telecentres improved individual and business opportunities for a select few. Being project-based, the management model was not significantly different from the Enda-Ecopop one. The difference was to be found in the objectives – to improve the business opportunities and performance of local businesses. So, although the TPS TCs were geared towards promoting business for their clients, they did not necessarily have to be good businesses themselves; they were after all fully funded "development projects". It is tempting not to come to the conclusion that as "a development project", what appears to have been perceived as an important and valued dimension of success is not financial sustainability but community participation.

Several conclusions can be drawn from this study:

- It is possible in contemporary society for disadvantaged individuals and community-based organizations to have access to valuable information in real time at affordable rates through the use of new ICTs.
- Telecentres offer social, economic, and cultural advantages, and the great enthusiasm for them is proof that they stand some chance of surviving and growing.
- The barriers to the use of ICTs, which are predicated on constraining factors such as illiteracy, gender, and age, can disappear with time and reasonable investments in models that encourage genuine community participation and capacity development. This investment ought to be the responsibility of a widening group of partners.

Chapter 8

Conclusion

This chapter examines the broad patterns that emerged from research conducted across 5 countries and 36 telecentres. The findings are examined in the light of the questions asked by the evaluation studies. The answers to these questions suggest possible evolutionary directions for community telecentres.

The four questions posed for these studies were related to issues of access, relevance, sustainability, and the environment within which the telecentres operate. This summary begins with a discussion of the social, political, economic, and technological environment in which the projects were implemented. This analysis provides the backdrop against which the projects can be understood, and from which extrapolations concerning their success or failure can be made.

The political, socio-economic, and technological contexts

The political environments within which the telecentres must survive are at this point in time not very positive. From Mali to Mozambique, the telecentre enjoys political support from a still small group of individuals. In Uganda, South Africa, and Senegal, and other African countries (e.g., Rwanda) support has come from the highest political levels in the country. Presidents Thabo Mbeki[1] of South Africa, Yoweri Museveni[2] of Uganda, and Abdoulaye

---

1 President Thabo Mbeki of South Africa is one of the architects of the Millennium Plan.
2 President Yoweri Museveni of Uganda was present at the Global Knowledge Conference in Canada and has continued to provide support for positive developments in the sector in Uganda.

Wade of Senegal[3] have, at various times in the past few years, made public statements in support of the development of information and communication technologies (ICTs) and by extension telecentres in their respective countries and in Africa. In October 2001, African leaders gathered in Abuja to put their countries individually and collectively on a path to sustainable growth and development in a landmark declaration called "A New Partnership for African Development." Section B of this historic document identifies sectoral priorities. Sections 99 through 111 highlight the need to bridge the infrastructure and digital divides, and elaborate the actions that must be taken. Five years earlier, in 1996, the United Nations, supported by 23 development organizations, launched a 10-year special initiative on Africa to encourage concrete actions to accelerate development on the continent. The African Information Society Initiative was part of this larger effort as was the Acacia Initiative aunched in 1997 as the Canadian government's response in support of the call for the African Information Society Initiative.

On a global level, there are currently numerous unilateral, multilateral, and private initiatives involved with the development and implementation of ICT projects. This process has been fuelled by cooperation and dialogue on a grand scale, epitomized by the two Global Knowledge conferences held in 1997 and 2000. Easily the most ambitious of these international efforts is the G8's Digital Opportunity Taskforce, (DOT Force). The DOT Force, nine-point action plan detailing a set of priority projects to be supported by countries and organizations for the promotion and development of ICTs has been handed over to the UN ICT Task force for implementation and continuity. Some countries have already commenced the implementation of some of the proposed plans.

These declarations and to a smaller extent actions suggest that some political support does exist for the development of ICTs in general. Although it appears that much of this action is still high-level political talk, these declarations could provide community telecentres the opportunity to grow. Nascent growth is taking place in some of the countries. In three of the five countries – South Africa, Mozambique, and Uganda – national ICT policies have either been enacted, or are being enacted, and it is reported that in about a third of the countries of the continent, NICI plans have been articulated. The high-level political support and goodwill towards ICTs in general do not translate at the

---

3 President Wade of Senegal promoted the Omega Plan, which emphasizes the development of ICTs as a tool for African growth, among others.

micro (telecentre) level with as much intensity. The politics and sociology of public access points suggests that they are designed and operated to cater for the needs of a geographically disadvantaged, economically weak and infrastructurally poor majority. This group is dispersed, ethnically and culturally diverse but significantly homogeneous in their involvement with agricultural occupations and among whom social capital and social asset building is valued. To what extent therefore is the community telecentre in its current form and structure aligned with these prevailing realities? In Senegal, and to a lesser extent in Uganda and South Africa, a few community telecentres provide a place of meetings and a resource for community action, information and education. But this dimension is not very well developed and it requires further examination and study because it does seem to make a difference in the disadvantaged communities in Dakar.

On the other hand, institutional transformation is progressing apace. In Mozambique, South Africa, and Uganda, independent and autonomous regulatory agencies have been created to catalyze developments in the telecommunications sector while in Mali and Senegal the regulatory institutions are semi-autonomous. Other noteworthy transformations in the telecommunications sector to date include the removal of state monopolies, the liberalization, and the continued haggling over privatization of telecommunications services. Still by 2000, the fixed telephone operations in Mali, Mozambique, and Uganda had not been privatized, although Uganda liberalized the sector permitting another operator to exist (ECA NICI 2000; UCC 2001) and a second network operator is being seriously considered in South Africa. In spite of the fact that privatization has commenced, state-owned or state-controlled telecommunications service providers still enjoy relative monopolies as well as exclusivity privileges in the five countries. No real competition exists for the provision of fixed-line services. On account of this absence of competition, tariffs remain high and infrastructure development in rural areas stultified. In contrast, the competition is in cellular and wireless telephony that in most countries of the continent has overtaken fixed or terrestrial telephony. Cellular and mobile telephony, spawned in all the five countries in the late 1990s, had by 1998 grown spectacularly and overtaken the number of terrestrial subscribers in three of the five countries (Senegal, Uganda, and South Africa) sometimes by margins of well over 100% (ECA NICI 2000). For example in 2000 the number of terrestrial lines in South Africa, Senegal and Uganda were: 2.1 million, 205,888 and 85,000, while the number of mobile subscribers in the same year were 9 million, 250,257 and 120,000 respectively (BMI-TechKnowledge 2002). The growth of mobile telephony indicates a yawning need that is still largely unmet and the need is greatest in the rural areas that have had very little telecommunications development. Yet mobile telephony is capable of bringing only small dividends since the current levels of wireless technologies available in the rural areas and what rural folk can afford will not bring the full benefits of the information age.

In addition to the telecommunications infrastructure, the general state of infrastructure continues to be a source of great difficulty in all five countries and to some extent most of the continent – particularly with regard to unreliable or non-existent telephone line connections and unreliable electricity supply. In Thakgalane, South Africa; for instance, the telecentre was not operating because there were no telephone lines. In some cases, such as in Buwama, Uganda, the basic telephone infrastructure was not available at the start of the project – a common occurrence in rural settings in the other African countries as well. Evidently universal rural access will not come easy. It was estimated that there were more than 10,000 registered telecentres in Senegal at the time of the study and most of them were concentrated in and around Dakar. In three of the other countries an exhaustive count or listing was difficult to make. In South Africa, 3,432 telecentres were identified in a Link Centre newsletter (*CommUnity* 2000) published by the University of Witwatersrand. The South African telecentres appear to have been spread over a wider area, a deliberate policy it seems, whereas, in the other four countries, the facilities, especially the private ones, and the infrastructure are concentrated in urban areas. In Uganda, for example, most of the services and the Internet service providers (ISPs) are concentrated in and around Kampala, as in Senegal.

Access: Emerging pictures

Users

What most ICT projects, and telecentres in particular, seek to do is democratize access to information and reduce the information gap and knowledge divide between the information haves and have-nots. The rationale for the creation of rural telecentres is based on the dichotomy in access between urban and rural populations and in the benefits of the information and networked age. Universal access is a commonly stated contemporary goal that addresses both the availability and affordability of information for all. The argument is made that, left to market forces only ICT services would not expand to poor rural communities. Indeed, the first generation information technologies (radio, television, and telephone) are still not widely available in much of rural Africa. Because rural poverty continues to be pervasive, public access points modelled around community telecentres are considered to hold the promise for reducing the urban–rural information divide. The profile of current users of telecentres is therefore an important indicator of the extent of their success in spreading benefits among rural populations.

User profiles in the five countries show broad similarities and a few differences. Undoubtedly, the telecentres have brought a large number of people in disadvantaged and under-served communities into direct contact with modern ICTs. This familiarization would not have been possible had the telecentre projects not been embarked upon in the first place (Graham 2001). Total numbers remain small in relation to total populations and users are shown to have been disadvantaged on the basis of age, gender, education, literacy levels, and socioeconomic status. A striking observation is the absence of old people at the telecentres. A number of reasons revolving around culture, human life-cycle development, and the nature and history of ICTs themselves surfaced from the focus group discussions to explain this pattern. The elderly, i.e., individuals over 50 years of age, were found to be significantly disadvantaged in Mali as in the other countries. In Mali, youth and adults younger than 40 years of age, constituted more than 80% of users. The most active telecentre users were between 17 and 40 years of age. In Uganda, about 71% of the users were between the ages of 18 and 50 years, and close to one-third (27.1%) were younger than 16 years old. The implication of this finding is that this new appetite for ICTs will remain for long.

Fewer women than men used telecentre services in practically all of the countries and facilities. In Mali, 77% of the users were men, and at Manhiça in Mozambique, 63% of the users were men. The trend in Senegal and Uganda was similar: in Uganda, 48.1% of users were male and in Senegal 70%. Only in South Africa were gender disparities in access different from the expected pattern: in Phalala, men constituted 42% of the total number of users. In the other South African telecentres the results were inconclusive. Some research seems to suggest that the sex of telecentre staff affects the gender nature of use. This notion requires further examination.

Education appeared to be a key determinant of telecentre use. A popular belief expressed by respondents, which was not fully confirmed by the data, reflected that telecentre services were for the elite or educated. In Mozambique, at least 50% of the users had secondary level education, and 63% of all users were students. In Uganda as in South Africa, university undergraduates, teachers and students made up the largest percentage of users. In Mali, speakers of Arabic were disadvantaged. Senegal, however, was exceptional in two respects: students were reportedly disadvantaged along with the poor and unemployed; and illiteracy did stop one using the TCs. This means that students who are considered educated did not use the community telecentres as much as other groups or as much as expected. The question would be why? One possible reason could be that the design and operation of the community TCs were skewed against this group by being closely focused on others. Students may also have had other more preferred alternatives since there were a huge number of TCs to chose from. We could therefore have had a situation of selective targeting by the community TCs that excluded students. The finding that poor and unemployed people were disadvantaged users of community telecentres is worrying and requires serious examination and drastic action. This is because by popular criteria a significant number of people fall into this category and unless they find utility for and in the TCs universal access will be difficult to claim.

In addition to the direct individual and institutional users, some telecentre benefits spread to a wider section of the population in the areas surrounding the telecentres. This seemed to feature prominently in Mali and Senegal and to a lesser extent in Uganda. The studies in the other countries did not assess this aspect of telecentre use, and information on secondary benefits requires further study.

Services

The telecentres in all five countries offered similar services: photocopying, telephony, and training in computer hardware, software, Internet access, and word processing. Facsimile transmission; document design, processing, and printing; and email services were also widely available. The range of services offered in the multipurpose community telecentres (MCTs) was wider than in the private telecentres or cybercafés. However, the level of use made of this wider array of services was lower. Low or non-use for some services was reported, for example the Internet and email in the more rural MCTs in Uganda, Mozambique, and Mali.

The huge popularity of the telephone is undisputed; however, there were small differences in the popularity of other services from country to country. Telephony accounted for no less than 50% of the income at all of the telecentres in Senegal and was more than 80% in some cases. In Senegal, in addition to telephony, Internet and email services were popular in the Trade Point Senegal TCs; whereas, in Mozambique and rural Uganda, email and Internet services were not very popular. Telephone, the most sought after service commonly suffered from connectivity problems. The reports suggest that telecommunications infrastructure problems in rural Uganda and South Africa were more severe than in the other countries. In Uganda and South Africa the sampled telecentres were in more rural areas than others and may, therefore, mirror more accurately the real challenges that ICT projects face in rural Africa.

Some of the MCTs in all countries provided other custom-made services. In Mozambique, Uganda, and Mali, the telecentres provided both print and electronic (videotapes, CD-ROMS, and audio tapes) resources for community use. Others had document holdings, resources or elaborate libraries as in Nakaseke in Uganda for the use of community members. The library and document service in the MCT in Nakaseke, Uganda, was the first library in the sub-county and had a marked effect on the surrounding community. Some of the Senegal MCTs offered web-site design, a service not offered by any of the other telecentres, but planned by some of the South African MCTs. The Timbuktu MCT was in the early stages of its transformation into an ISP equipped with a server and at the time of the study had up to ten customers.

A comparison of the services offered by MCTs and cybercafés showed that the range of services was wider in the development-oriented telecentres than in the profit-oriented cybercafés. The cybercafés had a very narrow service band and tended to specialize in communication (person-to-person) or information services (Jellema and Westerveld 2001). Given that the underlying ideologies for the two types of facilities were different, this is not surprising. The telecentres have a socioeconomic empowerment and development motive. A model of services can be extrapolated from that proposed by Jellema and Westerveld, which identifies three kinds of services, namely, communication, information and non-communication. According to this model, communication services include telephone, facsimile and computer mediated communication such as email. The second group of services includes 'information registration, consultation and receiving broadcasts' while the third group includes photocopying and computer related services. We believe that better labelling and expansion of the Jellema model to fit findings, in addition to theorizing the nature of the relationship between available and popular services on the hand, and the level of community development on the other, can improve this useful model.

It is possible therefore to identify the following groups of services:

- Communication (telephone, facsimile, email, chat, e-discussion etc.)
- Information (Internet surfing, radio broadcasts, newspapers, news bulletins, etc.)
- Education (Training, personal or group development exercises, transformation, etc.)
- Community development (village bulletin board, social centre/service, commercial service, i.e., sale of non communication, information and education services etc.).

In respect of the relationship between services and the level of community development, it is proposed that early in the evolution of TCs, simple communication, information and education services will dominate but as the clientele and the TCs evolve, more balance will develop to a point where a community TC will be providing not only more sophisticated services within each group but also the services will be spread strongly across at least three of the groups. It is hypothesized that the cybercafés, i.e., private TCs or access points on the other hand will continue to deliver services that are limited to one group in the name of specialization. The situation in all the countries suggests that not a high level of development has been attained in the service spectrum and it is believed that this is indicative of the age of the movement and the maturity of demand, which is itself related to the level of familiarisation (knowledge) with the tools.

Impediments to use

In this section, we present major impediments to the more widespread use of telecentres identified by respondents.

- **Inappropriate location.** Location greatly affected accessibility and the use of facilities in some of the telecentres. Additional costs, such as for transportation to get to the telecentre, and perceived threats to the user associated with the location, reduced use. For example, the Nabweru telecentre in Uganda is situated in the administrative centre of the sub-county in close proximity to a police station, a prison and magistrate's court. Some users found this threatening. Other potential users might be intimidated by public spaces or simply not have the freedom to be there as this may be considered culturally inappropriate. Most of the telecentres were housed in public buildings. In South Africa, Mankweng telecentre was located in an insecure area resulting in the loss of equipment to thieves. The same telecentre was also located in an area in which a number of facilities and businesses were providing similar services and consequently tough competition to the telecentre. However, striking a good balance may be easier said than done, e.g., location on a busy public road may be good for accessibility but bad from the point of view of noise, privacy, dust etc.
- **Poor publicity.** Closely tied to the inappropriateness of locations is poor publicity. Not enough seems to have been done to create awareness about either the locations of the telecentres or the services offered by them. For example, in Mankweng (South Africa) although the people were generally aware that a telecentre did exist, many did not know exactly where it was located. In Kampala city, a surprising number of people did not know where the neighbourhood cybercafé was to be found.
- **Poor management:** Most of the telecentres experienced some management problems, ranging from poor attitudes, to weak management, technical and even social skills. At some telecentres, the equipment was 'out of order', i.e., not working for long periods sometimes on account of bureaucratic delays. In Nabweru TC (Uganda) for example, the printer was not in use because there was no cartridge, and the telecentre had been waiting for the implementing and overseeing agency to authorize the purchase and eventual supply of cartridges for nearly three weeks. In Buwama, (Uganda) there was a history of long drawn difficulties between the management committee members and the telecentre staff, which affected the smooth delivery of services. In Makuleke (South Africa), poor financial and administrative management led to service interruption on account of huge unpaid bills.

The quality and number of staff was thought to be inadequate and marked by the use of poorly trained staff and volunteers with weak remunerations. In Uganda, as in many of the other MCTs, staff members were not adequately trained to deal with even routine technical problems. None of the TC mangers in Uganda was technically skilled to begin with although some basic training had been organized for them since becoming TC staff. The situation in Mali was different as the staff resolved most technical problems possibly because the executing agency is the national telecom operator.

Another dimension of poor management is reflected in TC working hours. The telecentres keep formal government working hours, which limit the time during which the facilities were open to the public. Facilities were usually not open at night, Sundays, or during public holidays, a fact that clearly shows that managers were not sensitive to profit making or customer sentiments.

- **Inadequate physical facilities.** In a number of cases, the available space was either too small or poorly managed. In most cases, there was little privacy for users of the telephones or other equipment. In Senegal as in other countries, the user-computer ratio during training was so large that classes had to be split and often the required practical (hands on) experience was impossible to meet.
- **Cost of equipment, maintenance and supplies.** The high cost of certain requirements, e.g., software licenses and cartridges for inkjet printers and the common practice of getting technicians from far away places for either routine maintenance or repairs interrupted use.
- **Cost of services.** Users in all the five countries expressed concern over the fees charged for services at the telecentres. The high cost of services in relation to earnings and incomes was identified as a serious barrier for women, the unemployed, and students.
- **Literacy and language.** Although the telecentres in Senegal, and to some extent Mali, were used by illiterates as much as by others, findings suggest that the telecentres were still perceived as places providing services for the educated. This perception is related to the language of the content most of which is in English or in French. In Senegal, the illiterate users received substantial assistance from the telecentre staff, and in both Senegal and Mali, business was conducted in the language of the surrounding environment.

Relevance of telecentres

It is often said that knowledge is power consequently the value of the services provided by the MCTs depends heavily on the type of content offered to the public. Relevance is considered in tandem with the kinds of services accessible through the MCT. Relevance can be evaluated on the basis of the value that users place on services, or the quality of content available in the telecentre. It is useful, therefore, to distinguish between the relevance of services on one hand and the value of content or applications on the other. It is also important to cast the discussion about relevance within a wider framework of a theory of ICTs for development. As a point of departure, it may be useful to develop an understanding of the linkages between services used and the purpose of use. Personal social or economic use can be distinguished from collective social, political and economic utility. Since community TCs are expected to play roles at both the personal and collective levels, relevance ought also to be evaluated from these standpoints.

The main reason for using the telecentres was to obtain or send information and the purpose of this information was for social interactions, for contacting friends and family, for preparing documents for social events (e.g., weddings and funerals), and for personal entertainment, such as watching television and videos, listening to radio, or reading newspapers. Professional and economic motives, such as seeking economic and agricultural information, came a distant second on the list of reasons for telecentre use. The telecentres facilitated business or commercial transactions for a small percentage of users in Uganda (10–20%). Information about improved or different farming practices and about prices for farm produce were given as reasons for use in Uganda; whereas, in Senegal and South Africa advertising for goods and services (e.g., domestic workers in Senegal), contacting business partners and buyers, and designing and photocopying company and institutional materials were also highlighted as motives. Students in Uganda and Mozambique and organizations in Senegal and South Africa used the telecentres for academic purposes: for processing documents (e.g., essays and newsletters), photocopying; for training in computer skills, web design, word processing, and key boarding; and for consulting various sources of information in the libraries.

Evidence from all the countries shows that the TCs in addition to having reached only a small percentage of all possible users, are predominantly accessed for personal social motives for maintaining family and other immediate contacts. It is hard to see how this type of use can lead to large-scale education or transformation if this is the desired end result. Collective social, political or economic utility is growing though still weak. The TCs played a visible role during the 2000 elections and in both Senegal and Uganda, some TCs were used as meeting places, for training groups of women, as places of shelter/safety etc. On a more pragmatic level, users expressed satisfaction with the services offered pointing out that the telecentres had opened them to wider audiences, facilitated external communication, and promoted knowledge of computer technology among local community members.

As regards the relevance of available content to local needs, there remains a huge unmet need. Despite the International Women's Tribune Centre's successful development of the CD-ROM *Rural Women in Africa: Ideas for Earning Money* (www.wougnet.org/news/cdupdate.html) efforts by other projects to develop content have not been too successful. Uganda had some success when the MCTs worked with local agricultural research agencies to repackage information for local farmers and agro-businesses (www.agricinfo.org). The Nakaseke MCT prepared and produced videos on a small number of issues, such as maize farming and mulching, developed a website featuring useful addresses, and kept newspaper cuttings of important events in the country. The Trade Point Telecentres in Senegal, created websites for local businesses and products. But no effort was made to bring all the developed websites together in a portal of local businesses or products. This might have attracted more browsing of the Internet.

The creation and use of applications in governance, health, education, for commerce, etc., was even less developed and the factors that obstruct the development of local content and applications include: the absence of relevant skills and expertise; the non-availability of funds; and the difficulties associated with cost recovery and user charges for information. For the most part information is usually passed free from one user to another. But there is growing evidence that with increased awareness, commercial activity and competition, agricultural information can be bought and sold.

Ownership, management, and sustainability

Contemporary development action considers that participation by local stakeholders is a necessary ingredient for the success and sustainability of initiatives and projects at community level. The case is made that participation improves local ownership, which engenders sustainability. Community ownership of telecentres was implied and vocally affirmed by key informants in all five countries. This was based on the fact that local community members were involved in some aspects of management in practically all of the telecentres in the study sample.

The extent of involvement of the local committees was not always clear and their level of responsibility often did not extend beyond supporting fund-raising and mobilization for the MCTs. One exception was the EIG Serbatim, Guédiawaye telecentre in Senegal. Most of the controlling muscle (management) was vested in the project-executing agencies, whether these were universities, as was the case in Mozambique, ministries or governmental agencies, as in Uganda and Mali, or NGOs as in South Africa. It is, therefore, masking the truth to say that the communities owned the telecentres. Ownership ought to confer control and evidently the local communities were not in control. Telecentre managers, who were usually employees of project executing agencies, often had more say in the affairs of the telecentres than the members of the management committees. Decisions affecting day-to-day management made by managers were usually cleared with the project implementing agencies before they could be effected – even when these were deemed fit and had been endorsed by local management committees.

Three ownership models were in evidence: private (individual) owned, private NGO or CBO owned and trusteeship. The franchise model seen in South Africa with the Universal Service Agency (USA) is regarded as a variant of private ownership. Most of the community TCs were in the category of trusteeship. This is an arrangement where the project is being held in trust by the executing agency for a specified period of time until the final owner, i.e., the community is ready to take it over. Although none of these ownership variations was found to be consistently associated with particular management outcomes, the private facilities tended to have clearer lines of authority, where as the most muddled were found in the trusteeship. The linkages and dynamics between the project funder/s (donor/s), the project proposer/implementer and local community actors were found to be complex and fuzzy as exemplified by the situation in Uganda (see chapter 5). This fuzziness affects management and makes the case for better illumination in the nature of significant relationships in the model through research a prerequisite for better understanding and possible refinement.

Fontaine and Fuchs (2000) propose a management typology that distinguishes three management models (adoption, municipal and commercial) which does not illuminate management patterns in a trustee model as found in the present study. In some of the telecentres (e.g., Nabweru, Buwama (Uganda), and Timbuktu (Mali)) the roles of the management committees were still not adequately explicit. It was unclear whether this was deliberate, so that the executing agencies could retain control over activities and budgets, or whether it was borne of a genuine lack of experience with successfully integrating and coordinating complex management structures involving local stakeholders. What was clear was the enthusiasm of community members to be more involved in the management of the MCTs. In Senegal, strong community support and a sense of collective ownership were apparent in some of the community telecentres. However, enthusiasm is no substitute for expertise, and whereas community members had plenty of enthusiasm, requisite skills in management (financial as well as technical) were grossly lacking among community members and to a lesser degree telecentre staff. Poor, unresponsive, or mediocre, management seemed to characterize most of the MCTs. The big question is 'does the trustee model by itself engender this kind of management?' Clearly more research is required to answer this question and to devise and implement a better management model, which guarantees sustainability.

A major debate concerning telecentres and public access points in general is the issue of financial sustainability. Are they viable enough to run on their own steam? The dimension of sustainability that is often considered of primary importance is financial sustainability and although it is important, the findings especially those in respect of relevance suggest that the issue is not so simple. The telecentres have been shown to have potential for sustainability on account of their social and cultural and the economic returns they provide for some users in Senegal. Services provided by the telecentres were greatly appreciated by community members. Some of the telecentres especially those located in disadvantaged neighbourhoods in Senegal, Uganda, and South Africa had become popular meeting places for community members and organizations. The telecentres had become a vital and integral part of the community social infrastructure. The point is made that telecentre sustainability depends on their successful integration into the community, their acceptance by the people, and the enthusiasm of the community to get involved in their management. It is therefore possible on the basis of this argument to distinguish institutional and conceptual validity from financial sustainability on the other. Arguments that seek to support the idea of the telecentre as a public good are seen as following this line of argument. But the eternal weakness of this position especially from the point of view of market logic is the fact that institutional and conceptual validity does not necessarily guarantee or translate into financial sustainability.

The financial sustainability of many of the community telecentres remains elusive. Even among private cybercafés, financial sustainability was not guaranteed for all facilities although more of them seemed to be making more profits than the community TCs. Two examples of sustainable community TCs were found in Phalala (South Africa) and Guédiawaye (Senegal). Whereas the basis of the financial success in Guédiawaye can be traced to the management and robust entrepreneurial style, the source and nature of the situation in Phalala other than it being one of the earliest TCs was unclear. Clearly more research needs to be done in this regard. The financial sustainability of the TC was under constant threat not only from weak management but also from recurrent technical and infrastructure problems in all five countries. The problems included: power failures or interruptions; poor connectivity; computer failures; printer breakdowns; non-functioning software; obsolete or unusable equipment; complex management arrangements, security failure and policy failures, e.g., import duties or taxes on equipment. Some telecentres in Uganda and Senegal, for example, had to go through considerable bureaucratic hurdles simply to have imported equipment released to projects or simply repaired. From available data it was apparent that the telecentres were not generating sufficient profits to be considered financially sustainable. However, it has been argued that the 'turn around' period for telecentres has yet to be reached because of their locations and the short time during which they have been operating. It has been suggested that three years is too short to expect the telecentres to be financially sustainable from the point of view of the evolutionary thesis advanced by Fuchs (1997). Another argument is that the initial objectives of the first generation telecentre projects were to demonstrate the pertinent issues and enable learning and not to prove financial sustainability. This has happened to a greater or lesser extent and in a matter of a few years, the story could be different and community telecentres could become popular and possibly sustainable. However, for this to happen the whole ideology of the telecentre movement needs to address inclusiveness, diversity, empowerment and self-reliance for all groups, users and non-users alike.

Conclusion: Whither community telecentres?

A logical conclusion for a book on telecentres is a look to the future. Are these strange new creations doomed to extinction, or will they evolve into a variety of new species, some of which may survive and perhaps flourish?

There is undeniably some political and social support for the development of ICTs on the African continent, and the telecentre model is considered to have merit and value for addressing the current disadvantage. The World Bank (2000) in its *Best Practice Review of Telecentres*, referred to the telecentre as:

> a promising new model for deployment of service to [marginalized] communities. It has been repeatedly declared that: information and communication technologies hold the promise of enormous positive influence on [African] countries' economic and social development (Conference of African Ministers of Finance, May 2001).

Great hope is placed on the potential of ICTs to speed the transformation of the continent.

However, political will and strong support must be translated into regulatory changes and financial commitments to improve the currently poor infrastructural and technological environments, which are prerequisites for the growth of telecentres. Decreases in direct foreign investments do not engender hope, although the liberalization of national telecommunication sectors and the rationalization and privatization of national telecommunications companies are providing opportunities for the inflow of financial resources. Developments in ICTs are being driven largely by the private sector and the related profit motive. A moderately equipped telecentre costs in the range of USD60,000–80,000 to establish and run as a project for about 2 years. The total cost to IDRC of two telecentres in Buwama and Nabweru was USD243,460 for 2 years and in South Africa the cost of one TC is said to be about USD16,000. The South African TCs were established on a franchise model with minimal investments in the physical structures that housed them and a limited (standard) number of equipment.

The financial performance of the African telecentres represented in this book is not very promising and is unlikely to ignite hope or interest for prospective and genuine private investors. It must however be borne in mind that the first generation TC projects did not set out to prove profitability or financial sustainability. Surprisingly, however, some telecentre staff (more than half of those asked in Uganda) indicated their preparedness to set up their own telecentre business if the opportunity presented itself. This seemed to be the strongest indication, in addition to the relative success of some of the community TCs and some private cybercafés, that community telecentres might yield reasonable returns on investments under appropriate conditions. The minimum of these conditions would appear to be ownership and management models different from the common 'trustee' one that appears to be most plagued by poor performance. Following the example in formal education where there is a range of arrangements, it is possible to see a similar scenario with community TCs where private, government and NGO/CBO owned facilities operate side by side. It is also possible to see the growth of arrangements involving multiple service providers in one physical location or facility.

One of the most basic conditions for the success of a community telecentre is an expansion of its clientele. With fewer than 50 users per month and an average of only 8 customers per week during the first year of operation of the well-resourced Timbuktu MCT, it is no wonder that profits cannot be made. Even considering the more current figures of 10–20 daily visits, only about 5,000 visitors would access the services at the telecentre in one calendar year, and this figure would include multiple visits by the same individuals. Much still needs to be done by the telecentres to expand their user base if they wish to improve the attractiveness of rural telecentres for prospective investors.

As a means to expanding the demand for their services, community telecentre and indeed the global telecentre movement, must concentrate on five critical Cs: Connectivity, Content, Capacity, Costs and a Conceptual framework. A framework that issues from a robust theory of ICTs for development and informs the imminent roll-out is an urgent necessity. This is of primary importance because without a framework anchored in the realities and genuine needs of the continent, any strategies developed to drive the spread and adoption of ICTs will fail as most afro-pessimists would say much else has from trade, industrialization and agriculture to formal education. If the roll-out is underpinned by a type of business plan centred around a market economy driven by a private sector framework, when most of the economies are not well developed optimally or fully functioning capitalist ones, the consequences in the long run will be underdevelopment or mis(sed)-development.

The spread should be based on a theory of social change, which treats all information as having potential value for instigating transformation and using the new technologies for spreading the most useful most widely. This means that the kinds and types of information that get collected, stored and disseminated should be those most valuable for the desired long term social change, not simply those that lead to short-term financial gains for a select group of individuals. To be certain, all members of society do not have the same opportunities to select what is valuable, but if the rule commonly intoned for "democracy" is used, then the voices of more people could be sought, heeded and used. To build or use a framework for ICT dispersal that does not take cognizance of the geography, ethno-linguistic diversity, the economic strength (or lack of) and the predominant occupational pattern of the majority of inhabitants of the continent is akin to navigating with a flawed compass. The consequences are predictable. A useful strategy would be to construct and use a framework that proceeds from the identified information and development needs of common folk as the base point from which to chart a path of transformation in whose service ICTs are applied. To do the reverse is tantamount to having ICTs lead people development. Although it does appear from time to time that the technologies are leading the developments and actions, an appropriate people-centred conceptual framework will bring clarity to the operations, and directions.

Connectivity is crucial for all e-transactions because, without it, the benefits of the new information and network age cannot be harnessed. But connectivity is beyond the direct control of telecentre operators or project implementers. Connectivity relies on the telecommunications infrastructure, which is provided or controlled by nation states, their agencies, or licensed private operators. Connectivity is also greatly affected by the quality of the electrical infrastructure because, without power, the equipment or hardware cannot operate. To ensure connectivity, simultaneous action is required on at least three fronts in addition to the involvement of a broad range of actors. These include the providers or controllers of the telecommunications and electrical infrastructures and the creators and producers of technology (hardware) and software. As the range of available technologies expands so, too, hopefully, will the costs continue to go down according to a popular law. The constraints imposed by the biophysical environments that characterize Africa need to be reflected in the technologies developed and diffused/adopted. Electricity and telephone networks remain the key to connectivity, yet solar energy abundant on the continent is still relatively untapped because the technology is so expensive.

Content and applications can be viewed as the blood that courses through the veins of connectivity or the electrical impulses travelling through a computer network. Local content is particularly valued but has been difficult to create. A good example of how to proceed with locally relevant content is provided by WorldSpace Foundation's Africa Learning Channel which sources content from existing local and international broadcast organizations and re-transmits same to a very wide audience using transmitters that cost less than USD100. Efforts to create local content for African telecentres are still in the incipient stages, but the demand is huge. If this important area is not addressed, the objective of linking telecentres with improvements in the livelihoods of the rural poor will be difficult to achieve. It is hard to imagine how successful e-commerce for continental businesses or e-governance for local authorities can occur if the businesses and governments have not established their own presence in cyberspace and changed their attitudes to email and/or Internet. It is imperative that a monumental effort aimed at collecting, creating, collating, transforming, and uploading relevant content be embarked upon immediately.

Recourse to the expertise that resides in older ICTs such as radio, television, and the print media (convergence) is being preached and seems like a promising way to go. To date the greatest difficulty with the creation or transformation of locally relevant and available content is human capacity. Local information is abundant, and continues to be generated in appreciable quantities by research centres, NGOs, individual researchers, journalists, and writers. The problem appears to be the expertise needed to convert predominantly print material into multi-media and digital formats that can be made readily accessible via computers on-line but more realistically off-line. This expertise and skills base needs to be created, expanded, and deepened across all social and occupational strata as a matter of urgency.

All the investments in connectivity, content, and capacity development will ultimately be meaningless if the cost of services is such that they remain unpopular, unreachable, or unusable by the large population of Africa's cash poor. For this reason all the costs associated with establishing and running telecentres must be reduced in order for the services to be provided at affordable rates to users. Government policies that influence costs and service pricing need to be implemented, e.g., import duties, taxes, broadcast operating licenses, e.g., VSAT etc, software and hardware prices, low-cost services, e.g., Voice Over Internet protocol (VOIP).

It makes simple economic sense to have a larger number of people use a service and pay a smaller amount than to have smaller numbers paying more. It makes sense to have policies that regulate and create order in the environment rather than having policies that strangle and frustrate operators. This leads to poor operations and weak investments in the required infrastructure. National policies need to support greater use and spread of required information, allow for low-cost telecommunication alternatives and remove barriers to small business development in the sector to bring services closer to the masses.

It makes sense to put money into training and capacity development to guarantee not simply sustainability but real development. It has been suggested that without human capacity development the gains of the information society cannot be harnessed by Africa.

The experiments in community telecentres described in this book show that weak and unsustainable models poor management and high establishment costs plague the young movement. On the other hand, the need for equity in access to the fruits of the contemporary boom in knowledge and information make the rural community telecentre a necessity. The rising rhetoric of rights, recalling the provisions of Article 19 of the "Declaration of Human Rights", the endorsement and adoption of the millennium development goals and other global documents provide rationales for supporting the telecentre movement. In all the countries where the demonstration has been mounted, the concept has received endorsement from users. This is the strongest evidence, if any is needed, to support its continued development and refinement.

The evidence presented in this book suggests that because rural and community telecentres are as important as schools and health clinics, they require support from development agencies and policy changes from national governments to guarantee their growth and evolution. It is hypothesized that this evolution will lead to the growth of a variety of facilities and models that will respond to the broad spectrum of business practice reflecting public ownership by governments, NGOs, or CBOs, franchises and full-fledged private ownerships. However to be meaningful to society, the growth in community telecentres and the spread of ICTs have to be grounded in an appropriate and relevant theory of social change hinged upon inclusiveness and relevance.

Appendix I
Contributors

Research teams
Mali
    Bah Babacar, Bureau d'Etudes de conseils et d'intervention au Sahel (BECIS)
    Sene Khamathe

Mozambique
    Cumbana Carlose
    Macome Esselina

Senegal
    Mor Dieng
    Pape Goumbalo Dione
    Paul Diouf
    Modou Faye
    Sidy Gueye
    Momar Mbaye
    Ndeye Gamou Mbodj
    Mansour Ndiaye
    Khamathe Sene
    Pape Touty Sow
    Amath Sy
    Mohamed Nabil Toure

South Africa
    Peter Benjamin

Christel Jacob
M. Lekoloane
Emelang Letean
Petunia Dolamo Motsaidi
Lettie Madibeng
M. Eddy Maepa
Jonas Maluleke
Kgatliso Masetlha
Sheila Mashao
Shadrack Mngomezulu
Lizzy Mokobane
Andrew Molefe
Kutu Mphahlele
Isaac Modibe Nkadimeng
Malefetjane Phineas Phaladi
Katharina Pillay
Rachel Basetsana Ramagogodi
S.C. Sebitsiwa
Sandra Ndhlovu Sefura
Sewela Sikhitla

Uganda
Samuel Kayabwe
Richard Kibombo
Esther Nakkazie
Stella Neema
Florence Etta
Sheila Parvyn-Wamahiu

Chapter 2
Contributions from Mike Jensen, Sheila Parvyn-Wamahiu

Partners
UNESCO (Hezekiel Dlamini and John Rose)
ITU
CODESRIA (Adebayo Olukoshi, Francis Nyamnjoh, Felicia Oyekanmi and Sulaiman Adebowale)

Acacia team
    Edith Adera
    Gado Alzouma
    Ronald Archer
    Alioune Camara
    Florence Etta
    Edward Holtcroft
    Heather Hudson
    Shafika Issacs
    Christel Jacobs
    Bas Kotterink
    Nigel Motts
    Ramata Molo Aw Thioune
    Frank Tulus
    Gaston Zongo

Acacia publications advisory committee
    Luis Barnola
    Fred Carden
    Bill Carman
    Laurent Elder
    Jean Marc Fleury
    Jennifer Pepall
    Terry Smutylo

Translation
    James Gichanga
    Xaverine Mukarusagara
    Maria Pavlidis

Editorial support
    Adetilewa Akin-Aina
    Sinmisade Akin-Aina
    Angela Etta
    Joanne Mwenda
    Irene K. Nyamu
    Eleanor Ochodo

Appendix II
Research questions

Access
- What types of ICTs are in telecentres?
- Which ICTs are used and for what? (Recreation, education, marketing, and subsistence).
- Who are the users and no-users? (Age, sex, education, and location).
- What impediments to use/access?
- How to surmount?

Relevance
- What services are on offer? Which ones are operational?
- What applications are available? Their relevance? Appropriateness?
- Satisfaction with services and applications?
- Experience of TC staff with creating applications?
- Required/Enabling conditions for creating attractive/relevant applications at local level?
- What approaches used for provision of services? Do they work?

Sustainability
- Ownership and management models in use? (Strengths and Weaknesses?)
- Scope and consequence of community participation in management?
- Partnerships to improve sustainability? How?
- What factors contribute to telecentre sustainability? (Economic, infrastructural, social, educational, political, and technical)
- Required capacities and capacity-building for sustainability?

Context/infrastructure
- Status of available technology/infrastructure?
- Sustainability of available technology? Available technology, useful and effective?

Appendix III

Research Instruments

This appendix provides short descriptions of the instruments used in three of the five countries (Senegal, Uganda and Mali). In each of these countries slight modifications were made of these instruments and in some instances not all of them were used. Three of the instruments borrowed heavily from those developed by PACT for the baseline survey conducted in the MCT Timbuktu in 1999.

Focus Group Discussion Guide

The guide includes a short list of questions used to ignite discussions and sustain them. The questions deal with the following issues:

- Information/Communication needs and issues.
- Priority Services
- Pricing
- Services-hours, atmosphere, support required/expected.

Document Analysis Guide

This guide seeks to assist the researcher in the systematic collection, organization and interrogation of documents, materials and resources at the telecentre. It suggests what to look for and what to do.

It provides suggestions on what resources and documents to search for and how to identify their relevance. It also suggests ways of handling the different types of documents which may be kept in the telecentre such as, user logs, reports and official documents, budgets and financial statements and suggestions for dealing with secondary information and documents such as govrenmnet publications.

The guide provides ideas on how to gender analyse documents by paying attention to language, illustrations etc.

Telecentre Usage Observation Guide

The main objective of the usage observation guide is to capture the nature of actual use made of the telecentre. This instrument is one of the genre of "naturalistic observation" which attempts to capture a slice of reality as it is happening. Observations are made of all people inside the telecentre at regular intervals, for example, every 15 minutes for a specified length of time in a specified period say one week.

The instrument, which consists of 12 columns, captures information in respect of services being used, those not, the age, gender and physical (handicapped) condition of users. The observation is conducted in a "fly on the wall manner", i.e., unobtrusively. Each observation is timed and all observations are expected to be of equivalent length. In the Uganda study for example each observation lasted about 2 minutes and many observations were made at regular times (morning and late afternoon) each day.

The key objects of observation are the users, their number, what they use and if they are assisted.

Telecentre Observation Guide

Although similar to the Telecentre Usage observation Guide, the Telecentre observation guide has as its objective focus the physical and social environment of the telecentre. This instrument was used to guide observations of the physical qualities and structure of the telecentre as well as record observable dimensions of user- staff relations. It consists of 23 items in 4 sections that deal with the identification of the place of observation, the layout or ground plan of the telecentre, the visible technology items and nature of client–staff relations. This instrument is intended to be used only once in a study.

Exit poll

A short Exit Poll was used for every nth user as s/he was leaving the telecentre to find out their impressions of the services they had used. Respondents are expected to state the adequacy, relevance, quality of services and their satisfaction with costs etc. in addition to stating what they would do if the telecentre were not in service or did not exist. In Uganda, for example, the instrument was administered to every 3rd female and every 3rd male user as they left the telecentre, or cybercafé.

Users were asked about the impact or difference the use or knowledge of computers had had on their lives e.g., if any jobs had been found as a result of learning to use telecentre computers.

Telecentre Questionnaire

The main objective of this instrument is to get detailed information on the telecentre.

It elicits historical, administrative (number, type of staff) and operational information such as type and size of tenement, number and type of equipment including furniture and energy source, services offered, the major problems encountered and how these are solved. It is completed by telecentre staff usually the manager and one instrument is completed for each telecentre.

Key Informant Interview Guide

There were six guides intended for representatives of the different groups of individuals involved with the telecentre, e.g., manager/staff of telecentre, committee member, local government official, service provider and project officer/programme officer and/or officer representing the implementing agency. The number and type of questions reflect the nature of involvement the informant has with the telecentre and the questions pursue a process and interaction focus eliciting information on administrative policies (at local, telecentre and central government levels) and practices.

In-depth Case Study Interview Guide

This is a detailed probe on the impact of telecentres on the user's household. It consists of 19 items.

The instrument solicits personal details of the user and her household as the context for telecentre use. The instrument seeks information on the nature of telecentre use (services, prices paid, regularity, length etc) and the impacts or benefits of this use on the respondent, her household members and circle of friends with whom the information is shared.

Individual Questionnaire

This typical survey instrument intended for a random sample of potential and actual users located within the vicinity of the telecentre consists of 23 items and seeks information about the information and communication needs of respondents and whether all the needs are satisfied by the telecentre.

Organizational Questionnaire

The organizational questionnaire was similar to the individual questionnaire with one major difference. Instead of individuals, it was used to identify organizations' information needs and their usual strategies for dealing with these.

Bibliography

ACACIA, 1997, 'Evaluation and Learning System for ACACIA': A report based on a Consultative Meeting Held in Johannesburg, February 12–14 1997 http://www.idrc.ca/acacia/03230/16-els

Adedeji, A., ed., 1993, *Africa Within the World*, London, Zed Books Ltd.

Adera, E. and Etta, F., 2001, *Information Communications Technologies (ICTs) in Africa*, Paper presented at the workshop for media women, Gigiri, UNESCO.

Adera, E.O. and Rathgeber, E.M., eds., 2000, *Gender and the Information Revolution in Africa*, Ottawa, IDRC.

Adeya, C.N., 2001, *Information and Communication Technologies in Africa: A Selective Review of Studies and Projects*, United Kingdom, International Network for the Availability of Scientific Publications (INASP).

Africa Union, 2001, *A New African Initiative—Merger of the Millennium Partnership for the African Recovery Programme (MAP) and Omega Plan*.

African Development Bank, 2001, 'Basic Indicators on African Countries—Comparisons', (http://www.afdb.org/african_countries/information_comparison.htm).

Agha S.S., 1992, *Sustainability of Information Systems in Developing Countries—An Appraisal and Suggested Courses of Action*, Ottawa, International Development Research Centre (IDRC).

Akhtar, S. (ed.), 1990, *National Information and Informatics Policies in Africa Report and Proceedings of a Regional Seminar*, Ottawa, International Development Research Centre (IDRC).

Alcantara, C.H., 2001, *The Development Divide in a Digital Age—an Issues Paper*, Paper No. 4, Geneva, UNRISD.

APC, 1997, *APC Africa Strategy Development Meeting Report*. Commissioned by IDRC/Acacia, Johannesburg, South Africa, (http://www.idrc.ca/acacia/outputs/op-apc.htm)

Banks, K. and Ramilo, C.G. (undated) *Lessons Learned—Building Strong Internet Based Women's Networks.* Final Narrative Report by the Association for Progressive Communications (APC) Women's Networking Support Programme (WNSP).

Baron, L.F. 1999, 'Experiments in Community access to New Communication and Information Technologies in Bogota' in Gomez R. and Hunt P. (eds).

Benjamin P., 2000, 'ICT projects in South Africa'. *CommUnity,* Volume

Benjamin P., 2000, *Northern Province Telecentre Community Research.* Commissioned by IDRC/Acacia, Johannesburg, South Africa.

Benjamin, P and Dahms, M. 1999, 'Socialise the Modem of Production- The Role of Telecentres in Development' in Gomez R. and Hunt P. (eds).

Bhalla A.S., ed., 1998, *Globalization, Growth and Marginalization*, Ottawa and Oxford, IDRC/Macmillan.

Biswas S., 2001, *Digital Empowerment: Seeds of E-Volution*, Outlook (http://www.india.com).

Blau, A., 2001, 'More Than Bit Players: How Information Technology Will Change the Ways Nonprofits and Foundations Work and Thrive in the Information Age'. A Report to the Surdna Foundation, New York.

BMI-TechKnowledge, 2002, *Communications Technologies Handbook,* South Africa, BMI_TechKnowledge Group.

Bopp, M., Gandaho, D, Guideme A., Neufeld, R., and Soude T., 1997,. *Making Connections—An Assessment of the Information and Communication Technology Needs of CREDESA for HealthCare Work in the Ouidah District of Benin.* Commissioned by IDRC/Acacia, (http://www.idrc.ca/acacia/outputs/op-cred.htm)

Bridges.org, 2001, *Spanning the International Digital Divide,* (http://www.bridges.org)

Byron I. and Gagliardi R., 2001, *Communities and the Information Society – The Role of Information and Communication Technologies in Education in Education,* (http://www.idrc.ca/acacia/outputs/op-apc.htm)

Camacho, K., 2000, *Research into the Impact of the Internet on Civil Society Organizations in Central America*, (http://www.idrc.ca/pan/panlackemdoc1_e.htm)

Chale, E.M., 1997, *Distance Learning for Change in Africa, A Case Study of Senegal and Kenya, Policy and Research Prospects for IDRC, Acacia.* Ottawa, International Development Research Centre (IDRC).

Cisler et al, 1998, 'Computer and Communications Use in Low-Income Communities' in Gomez R. and Hunt P. (eds) (1999).

Conference of African Ministers of Finance, 2001, *Ministerial Statement, 10 May*, Algiers, Algeria (http://esa.un.org/ffd/policydb/PolicyTexts/eca-4.htm)

Cryderman, K., 2001, *Latin American Telecentres: The Community Networking Pilot Project,* Reports: Science From The Developing World, Ottawa, International Development Research Centre (IDRC).

CSIR, 2001a, *Report 1: Monitoring and Evaluation of Libraries as Gateways to Information in Africa*, Council for Scientific and Industrial Research, Division of Information and Communication Technology, Johannesburg, Regional Office for Southern Africa, IDRC, ROSA.

CSIR, 2001b, *Report 2: Monitoring and Evaluation of Libraries as Gateways to Information in Africa*, Council for Scientific and Industrial Research, Division of Information and Communication Technology, Johannesburg, Regional Office for Southern Africa, IDRC, ROSA.

Dahms, M. 1999, 'For the Educated only... Reflections on a visit to two Multipurpose Community Telecentres in Uganda' in Gomez R. and Hunt.

Dandar, N. 1999, 'Establishing\ a Public internet Centre in Rural Areas of Mongolia' in Gomez R. and Hunt P. (eds).

Day, P. and Harris, K., 1998, *Down-to-Earth Vision. Community-Based IT Initiatives and Social Inclusion.* IBM Community Development Foundation, (http://www.ids.ac.uk/eldis/hot/north.htm)

Delgadillo, K. and Borja, R. (undated) *Learning Lessons from Telecentres in Latin America and the Caribbean*, (http://www.idrc.ca/telecentre/evaluation/nn/16_Lea.html)

DFID, 2000, *Making Globalisation Work for the World's Poor: An Introduction to the United Kingdom Government's White Paper on International Development*, London, DFID.

DOT-Force, 2001a, *Creating a Development Dynamic – Final Report of the Digital Opportunity Initiative*, (http://www.opt-init.org/framework.html)

DOT-Force, 2001b, *Digital Opportunities for All: Meeting the Challenge.* Report of the Digital Opportunity Task Force (Dot Force), 11 May.

ECA, 1996, *Keynote address by Dr. K.Y. Amoako, Executive Secretary, ECA, South Africa,* AISI Conference: Empowering Communities in the Information Society. Addis Ababa, Ethiopia, UNECA.

ECA, 2000, *NICI Indicators: An Overview of the African ICT Sector 1998/99,* (http://www.uneca.org/aisi/nici/nici%20indicators.htm)

ECA, 2001, *AISI ADF '99 Report / ADF'99 Post Forum Summit*, Addis Ababa, Ethiopia UNECA.

Editorial, 2001, *Harnessing Information and Communication Technologies for a More Sustainable Future*, St. Georges House, Windsor Castle, (http://www.mandamus.co.uk/bshf/publications/stgeorge/harnessing_it/cover.html)

Etta, F.E., Agonga, A., and Katia, S., 2001, *Acacia in Kenya – A Study of Information and Communication Technologies and Community Development: Final Research Report*, Nairobi, International Development Research Centre (IDRC).

Etta, F.E., 2000, *Revised Concept Paper for the African Telecentre Study*, Nairobi, IDRC.

Etta, F.E., Kibombo, R., Kayabwe, S.K., Nakkazi, E., Neema, S., and Parvyn-Wamahiu, S., 2001, *Panafrican Telecentre Study (Uganda Component)*, Nairobi, IDRC.

Faye, M., 1998, *Telematics Policies in the African Context*, (http://www.unesco.org/webworld/build_info/rinaf/docs/telematics_policies_makane_faye.html)

Fillip Barbara, 2002 ,'ICTs for disadvantaged Children and Youths - lessons from Brazil and Ecuador', *Techknowlogia* July-Sept,

Fontaine, M with R. Fuchs, 2000, 'The watering hole; creating learning communities with computers', *Techknowlogia,* May/June.

Foster, M., 2001, *ICTs Help to Empower Women in Poor Areas*, (http://www.iconnect-online.org/)

Fuchs, R., 1997, *If You Have a Lemon, Make Lemonade: A Guide to the Start-Up of the African Multipurpose Community Telecentre Pilot Project*, Ottawa, International Development Research Centre (IDRC), (http://www.idrc.ca/acacia/outputs/lemonade/lemon.html)

Fuchs, R., 1998, *Little Engines That Did: Case Histories from the Global Telecentre Movement* (http://www.idrc.ca/acacia/engine/)

Gigler, B.S., 2001, *Empowerment Through the Internet Opportunities and Challenges for Indigenous Peoples*, TechKnowLogia, Vol. 3 (Issue 4), (http://www.techknowlogia.org/TKL_active_pages2/TableOfContents/main.asp?IssueNumber=12)

Gomez, R. and Martinez, J., 2001, *The Internet Why? And What For?* Ottawa, International Development Research Centre (IDRC).

Gomez, R. and Martinez, J., 2000, *Beyond Connectivity: New Information and Communication Technologies for Social Development* (http://www.idrc.ca/pan/pubacceso5_e.htm)

Gomez, R., Martinez, J., and Reilly, K., 2001, *Paths Beyond Connectivity – Pushing the Limits of Information and Communication Technologies for Development*, Ottawa, IDRC.

Gomez, R. and Hunt, P. (eds.), 1999, *Telecentre Evaluation: A Global Perspective, Report of an International Meeting on Telecentre Evaluation*, Ottawa, IDRC.

Gomez, R., Hunt, P., and Lamoureux, E., 1999, *Enchanted by Telecentres: A Critical Look at Universal Access to Information Technologies for International Development*, College Park, University of Maryland.

Government of the United Kingdom, 2000, *Eliminating World Poverty: Making Globalisation Work for the Poor*, White Paper on International Development (http://www.globalisation.gov.uk/)

Graham, M., 1997, *Use of Information and Communication Technologies in IDRC Projects: Lessons Learned*, Ottawa, IDRC. (http://www.idrc.ca/acacia/outputs/op-eval.htm)

Graham, M., 2001, *Evaluation and Learning System for Acacia (ELSA): Emerging Lessons*, Ottawa, IDRC.

Hafkin, N., 1998, *First International Conference on Rural Telecommunications Reports and Presentations*, AISI, Addis Ababa, UNECA, (http://www.ntca.org/intlconf/rapgen11.html)

Hafkin, N., 2001,'Gender, information Technology and the digital divide in Africa', The World Bank Group Gender and the digital divide seminar series # 6, March.

Hamilton, P., 2002, The African Communications Infrastructure and Services Report 2002 / 03, AITEC.

Hamilton, Paul, 2002, 'Broadband Access: Connecting the last mile' *Computers and telecommunications in Africa 16,5,38,42*.

Hammond, B., 2001, *OECD Global Forum on Knowledge Economy. Summary Record of the Joint OECD/UN/UNDP/World Bank Global Forum – Exploiting the Digital Divide Opportunities for Poverty Reduction*. Paris, Organization for Economic Co-Operation and Development (OECD).

Harfoush, N. *Acacia Information and Telecommunications Technology Issues*, Ottawa, Ottawa, IDRC. (http://www.idrc.ca/acacia/outputs/op-issu.htm)

Horak, R., 2001, *Telecommunications Technology Essentials: Technology in Context*, Mt. Vernon, WA. The Context Corporation.

Harris, R. W., 1999, 'Evaluating Telecentres within National Policies for ICTs in Developing Countries' in Gomez R. and Hunt P. (eds)

Hudson, H.,1999, 'Designing Research for Telecentre Evaluation' in Gomez R. and Hunt P (eds)

Huyer, S., 1997, *Women in Global Science and Technology (WIGSAT): Supporting Women's Use of Information Technologies for Sustainable Development*, Ottawa, Gender and Sustainable Development Unit, IDRC. (http://www.idrc.ca/acacia/outputs/womenicts.html)

Huyer, Sophia, 2002, 'The Leaky Pipeline: Gender Barriers in Science, Engineering and Technology', Presentation at the World Bank Group, Gender and Digital Divide Seminars # 15, February

IDRC, 1996, *Information and Communications Technologies (ICTs) and Governance: Linkages and Challenges*, Ottawa, IDRC. (http://www.idrc.ca/acacia/studies/ir-gove.htm)

IDRC/Acacia, 1999, *The Wireless Toolbox: A Guide to Using Low-Cost Radio Communication Systems for Telecommunication Developing Countries – An African Perspective*, Ottawa, IDRC. (http://www.idrc.cà/acacia/03866/wireless)

Henault, G., 1996, *Employment and Income Generating Activities Derived From Internet Access*, Ottawa, IDRC. (http://www.idrc.ca/acacia/studies/ir-henlt.htm)

InfoDev, 1998, *Global Connectivity for Africa: Key Issues for Decision Makers*, Addis Ababa, Ethiopia, The Information for Development Programme (InfoDev).

Intelecon Research and Consultancy Ltd., 2001, *Policies and Strategies for Rural Communications in Uganda*, Nairobi, IDRC.

ITDG, 2001a, *Technology, Poverty and the Future of the Developing World: An ITDG Seminar Report*, Imperial College, London, Intermediate Technology Development Group.

ITDG, 2001b, *An ITDG Special Response to the Human Development Report 2001: Which Technologies Most Benefit Poor Women and Men?* London, Intermediate Technology Development Group (ITDG).

ITU, 1998a, *Integrated Rural Development and Universal Access: Brief Description of ITU's Buenos Aires action Plan*, Programme No. 9 and 12, Geneva, International Telecommunications Union (ITU).

ITU, 1998b, *Telecottage and Telecentre Survey*, Geneva, International

Telecommunications Union (ITU), (http://www.itu.int/ITU-D/univ_access/seminar/buda/proceedings/Budapest-en.pdf)

ITU, 1999, *World Telecommunication Development Report*, Geneva, International Telecommunications Union (ITU).

ITU, 2001a, *ITU Internet Country Case Studies—Uganda*, Geneva, International Telecommunications Union (ITU), (http://www.itu.int/ti/casestudies/uganda/uganda.html)

ITU, 2001b, *ITU Internet Country Case Studies: Overview*, Geneva, International Telecommunications Union (ITU) (http://www.itu.int/ti/casestudies/overview.html)

Jellema, J and Rudi Westerveld, 2001, 'Learning lessons from failure: the Ugandan telecentre experience in prospective' ITU Telecom Africa, November.

Jensen, M., 1996a, *Bridging the Gaps in Internet Development in Africa*, Ottawa, IDRC (http://www.idrc.ca/acacia/studies/ir-gaps.htm)

Jensen, M., 1996b, *A Guide to Improving Internet Access in Africa with Wireless Technologies*, Ottawa, IDRC, (http://www.idrc.ca/acacia/studies/ir-jens.htm)

Jensen, M., 1998, *Where is Africa on the Information Highway? The Status of Internet Connectivity in Africa.* (http://www.unesco.org/webworld/build_info/rinaf/docs/cari98.html)

Jensen, M., 2000, *African Internet Connectivity: Information and Communication Technologies (ICTs) Telecommunications, Internet and Computer Infrastructure in Africa* (http://www3.sn.apc.org/)

Jensen, M., 2001, *African Internet Connectivity, 2001* (http://www3.sn.apc.org)

Karelse, C. M. and Sylla-Seye F., 2000, 'Rethinking Education for Production, use and Management of ICTs' in Rathgeber E.M. and Adera E.O. (Eds)

Kelly, T. and Minges, M., 2001, *Around the World*. ITU News, International Telecommunications Union (ITU).

Kinyanjui, W.G., 2001, *Building Information Community in Africa*. Paper presented at the Kenya Information Society Workshop, Nairobi, Kenya, 13–14 October.

Knoch, C., 1997, *Uninet: The South African Academic and Research Network*. Ottawa, IDRC/Acacia (http://www.idrc.ca/acacia/outputs/op-unin.htm)

Kyabwe, S and Kibombo R, 1999, 'Buwama and Nabweru Multipurpose Community Telecentres: Baseline Surveys in Uganda' *in* Gomez R. and Hunt P.(eds)

Latchem, C. and Walker, D., 2001, *Perspectives on Distance Education, Telecentres: Case Studies and Key Issues*, Vancouver, The Commonwealth of Learning.

Leon O., Bruch, S. and Tamayo, E., 2001, *Social Movements on the Net*, Quito, Agencia Latino Americana de Information.

Levin, L., 1996, *Report to IDRC on the Use of Information and Communications Technologies (ICTs) in Sub-Saharan Africa in the Area of Governance*, Johannesburg, SangoNet.

Loum, M. and Lamine, M. (undated) *The New Information Technologies and Trade*, Dakar, Trade Point Senegal.

Louw, K., 1996, *The Use of Information and Communication Technologies (ICTs) that Add Value to Development Programmes in Sub-Saharan Africa: Employment Report*, CSIR Information Services, (http://www.idrc.ca/acacia/studies/ir-csir.htm)

Macome, E. and Cumbana, C., 2001, *Assessment Study of Manhiça and Namaacha Pilot Telecentres*. Maputo, Commissioned by International Development Research Centre (IDRC).

Maepa M.E., Molefe, A., and Ramagogodi, R., 2001, *Bakgaga-Ba-Mothapo Multi-Purpose Centre*, Report to IDRC/Acacia, Nairobi, IDRC.

Mansell, R. and When, U., 1998, *Knowledge Societies for Sustainable Development*, Oxford, Oxford University Press.

Mansell, R. and Crede, A., 1998, *Knowledge Societies in a Nutshell*, Ottawa, IDRC.

Marker, P., McNamara, K., and Wallace, L., 2001, *The Significance of Information and Communication for Reducing Poverty*, Development Policy Department, DFID Final Report, London, DFID.

Martinez, J., 2000, *Central America: National Environments for Internet Access*, Pensando las politicas publicas, No. 7, (http://www.idrc.ca/pan/pubacceso7_e.htm)

Mayanja, M., 2000, *Access and Empowerment: Experience and Lesson from The Multi-Purpose Community Telecentres (MCT) in Uganda*, Paper presented at The Second Global Knowledge Conference (GKII), Kuala Lumpur, Malaysia.

McChesney R.W., Wood, E.M, and Foster, J.B. (eds.), 1998, *Capitalism and the Information Age: The Political Economy of the Global Communication Revolution*, New York, Monthly Review Press.

Menou M.J., 1999, *Synthesis Report, Part 1: Methodological Issues. Connectivity in Africa: Use, Benefits and Constraints of Electronic Communications*, Ottawa, IDRC.

Morna L. and Khan, Z., 2000, *Net Gains*, Gender Links, June.

Mulyampiti, T., 2001, *New Information and Communication Technologies (NICS) and Governance in Uganda*. Paper presented at the Centre for Basic Research, Seminar Room, April.

Mureithi, Muriuki, 2002, 'Ushering East Africa into the global information society: telecommunications policy imperatives for the next phase of development', paper presented at the East African Telecoms and Broadcasting Conference, EA Telecom 2002, KICC, Nairobi, Kenya.

Mureithi M., Ghenna, K., Misubire, V., and Mullin, J. (eds.), 2001, *The ECA/IDRC Pan-African Initiative on E-commerce: Regional Report on East Africa*, January.

Nath, V., 2000, *Heralding ICT Enabled Knowledge Societies: Way Forward for the Developing Countries*, (http://www.members.tripod.com/knownetwork/articles/heralding.htm)

NEPAD, 2001, *The New Partnership for Africa's Development*, South Africa, Department of Foreign Affairs, (http://www.dfa.gov.za/events/nepad.pdf)

Nordicity Group Ltd., 1997, *Community Experiences with Information and Communications Technology-Enabled Development in Canada – Local Experiments in Innovation*, Commissioned by ICT Branch, Ottawa, IDRC.

Nostbakken, D. and Akhtar, S., 1994, *Does The Highway Go South? Southern Perspectives on The Information Highway*, Pre-Conference Symposium on Southern Country Interests, Tampere, Finland.

Northern Province: Thakgalane Community Telecentre Report. (undated) South Africa.

Northern Province: Botlokwa Community Telecentre Report. (undated) SA.

Northern Province: Phalala Community Telecentre Report. (undated) SA.

Northern Province: Mankweng Community Telecentre Report. (undated) South Africa.

NTCA (undated) *Initial Lessons Learned About Private Sector Participation in Telecentre Development,* Arlington, National Telecommunications Cooperative Association.

NUA Internet Surveys, 2001, *How Many Online?* (http://www.nua.ie/surveys/how_many_online/)

Ochodo, E., 2001, *Report on Information and Telecommunications Technology (ITs) and the Telecommunications Landscape in Africa*, Ottawa, IDRC.

OECD and IDRC, 2001, *Donor Information and Communication Technology (ICT) Initiatives and Programmes*. Joint OECD/UN/UNDP/World Bank Global Forum Exploiting the Digital Opportunities for Poverty Reduction, Paris, OECD.

Patton, M.Q., 1997, *Utilization-Focused Evaluation: The New Century Text*, London, Sage Publications.

Powa, M., 1997a, *Private Sector Learning Centre Partnerships*, Commissioned by IDRC/Acacia, Midrand, South Africa.

Powa, M., 1997b, *Exploring a Basic Illiterate Web Access System: Discussion and Demonstration of Technical Concepts, and Pointers to Future Research,* Ottawa, IDRC. (http://www.idrc.ca/acacia/outputs/op-audi.htm)

Press, L., 1996, *The Role of Computer Networks in Development*, Communications of the ACM, Vol. 39, No.2, (http://som.csudh.edu/fac/lpress/devwins.htm)

Press, L., Burkhart, G., Foster, W., Goodman, S., Wolcott. P., and Woodard, J., 1998, *An Internet Diffusion Framework*, Communications of the ACM, Vol. 14, No. 10 (http://som.csudh.edu/fac/lpress/articles/acmfwk/acmfrwk.htm)

Proenza, F.J., Buch, R.B., and Montero, G., 2001, *Telecentres for Socioeconomic and Rural Development in Latin America and the Caribbean*, Washington, DC, Inter-American Development Bank (http://www.iadb.org/sds/itdev/telecenters/index.htm)

Robinson, S., 2001, *Rethinking Telecentres: Knowledge Demands, Marginal Markets, Microbanks And Remittance Flows*, e-OTI: On the Internet, March/April (http://www.isoc.org/oti/).

Rathgeber E.M. and Adera E.O., (Eds) 2000, *Gender and the Information Revolution in Africa,* IDRC, Ottawa, Canada.

Rathgeber E.M, 2000, 'Women, Men and ICTs in Africa: Why Gender is an Issue' in Rathgeber E.M. and Adera E.O. (Eds)

Sagna, O., 2000, *Information Technologies and Social Development in Senegal*, UNRISD News, No. 23. Autumn/Winter.

Schlemmer, L. and Smith, J., 2001, *Rural Business Information Network*

Project. Project Documentation. Final Report: Analysis of the Project Progress, Performance and Possibilities, Ottawa, IDRC.

Sene, K., 2001, *Panafrican Study on Telecentres in Mali, MCT of Timbuktoo*, Commissioned by IDRC, Senegal, IDRC.

Sene, K., Sow, P.T., and Dieng Mor, 2001, *Panafrican Study on Telecentres, Senegal*, Commissioned by IDRC, Senegal, IDRC.

Shirley, M.M, Tusubira, F.F, Gebreal F. and Huggarty, L., 2002, 'Telecommunications Reform in Uganda' Policy research Working Paper 2864, The World Bank Dev.Reg. Grp.

Shiroya, F. and Ongeso, R. (eds.), 1997, *IDRC-Kenya Schoolnet Workshop, Proceedings of a Workshop held in Lenana Mount Hotel*, Nairobi, IDRC.

Skuse, A. (undated) *Information Communication Technologies, Poverty and Empowerment* (http://www.imfundo.org/knowledge/skuse.htm)

Stavrou, A., Benjamin, P., Burton, P., and McCarthy, C., 2000, *Telecentres 2000: The Way Forward* (http://www.communitysa.org.za/docs2/t2000_synth.doc)

Tulus, F., 1999, *Annotated List of Reports from Commissioned Studies in Acacia*, Acacia/IDRC, Ottawa, IDRC.

Uday, M., 2000, *Bridging the Digital Divide*, 2020 Vision, News and Views, September, Washington, DC., International Food Policy Research Institute (IFPRI) (http://www.ifpri.org/)

Uganda Communications Commission, 2001, *Rural Communications Development Policy for Uganda*, Kampala, Uganda Communications Commission (UCC).

Uganda Bureau of Statistics, 2001, *Uganda National Household Survey 1999/2000: Report on the Community Survey*, Kampala, Uganda Bureau of Statistics.

UNCST, 2001, *National Information and Communication Technology Policy Framework for Uganda*, Kampala, Uganda National Council for Science and Technology.

UNDP, 2001, *Human Development Report 2001: Making New Technologies Work for Human Development*, New York, United Nations Development Programme (UNDP) (http://www.undp.org/hdr2001/)

UNDP, 2002, *Driving Information and Communications Technology for Development: A UNDP Agenda for Action 2000–2001*. New York, United Nations Development Programme (UNDP) (http://www.sdnp.undp.org/it4dev/ffICTe.pdf)

UNECA African Development Forum, 1999a, *Globalization and the Infor-*

mation Economy: Challenges and Opportunities for Africa, Addis Ababa, United Nations Economic Commission for Africa (UNECA), (http://www.uneca.org/adf99/docs.htm)

UNECA African Development Forum, 1999b, *Strengthening Africa's Information Infrastructure*, Addis Ababa, United Nations Economic Commission for Africa (UNECA) (http://www.uneca.org/adf99/infrastructure.htm)

UNECA African Development Forum, 1999c, *The Process of Developing National Information and Communications Infrastructure (NICI) in Africa*, Addis Ababa, United Nations Economic Commission for Africa (UNECA), (http://www.uneca.org/adf99/nici.htm)

UNECA, 1999, *Developing National Information and Communications Infrastructure (NICI) Policies, Plans and Strategies: The "Why" and "How"*, Addis Ababa, United Nations Economic Commission for Africa (UNECA) (http://www.anais.org/ARTICLES/DOC20.HTML)

UNECA, 2000a, *Status of Information and Communication Technologies in Africa: The Changing Regulatory Environment*, Addis Ababa, United Nations Economic Commission for Africa (UNECA), (http://www.uneca.org/aisi/nici/status_of_information_and_commun.htm)

UNECA, 2000b, *What is AISI?* Addis Ababa, United Nations Economic Commission for Africa (UNECA) (http://www.uneca.org/aisi/docs/what'sAISI.PDF)

UNESCO, 2000. *Only 4% of the Internet Users in the Arab World Are Women*, Paris, United Nations Educational, Scientific and Cultural Organization (UNESCO) (www.unesco.org/webworld/news/000605_beijing.shtml)

UNESCO, 2001a, *International Seminar on Digital Divide Opened in Sri Lanka*, Paris, United Nations Educational, Scientific and Cultural Organization (UNESCO) (http://www.unesco.org/webworld/news/2001/010123_kothmale.shtml)

UNESCO, 2001b, *The Telecentre Cookbook for Africa. Recipes for Self-Sustainability: How to Establish a Multi-Purpose Telecentre in Africa*, Paris, United Nations Educational, Scientific and Cultural Organization (UNESCO),(http://unesdoc.unesco.org/images/0012/001230/123004e.pdf)

UNICEF (WCARO), 2001, *Girls Education: Regional Strategy for West and Central Africa (Draft 2)*, Abidjan, West and Central Africa Regional Office, United Nations Children's Fund (UNICEF).

Unuth, R.T., 1995, *Telematics Strategy for Africa: The Case of Mauritius* (http://www.sas.upenn.edu/African_Studies/Padis/telmtics_Unuth.html)

US Department of Commerce, Office of Telecommunications, 1999, *Status of Telecommunications Privatization and Sector Reform in Sub-Saharan Africa*.

Van Heusden, P., 1996, *A Survey of Information Communication Technology in Sub-Saharan Africa*, Ottawa, IDRC. (http://www.idrc.ca/acacia/studies/ir-heus.htm)

Wamahiu, S.P., 2001, *Telecentre Study: Review of Literature*, Nairobi, IDRC.

Wilson, E.J. *Closing the Digital Divide: An Initial Review*, Internet Policy Institute (http://www.internetpolicy.org/briefing/Ernest Wilson0700.html)

World Bank, 1993, *Uganda Growing Out of Poverty*, Washington, DC, The World Bank.

World Bank, 2000a, *Best Practice Review of Telecentre Operations*, Washington, DC, The World Bank.

World Bank, 2000b, *Can Africa Claim The 21st Century? Overview*, Washington, DC, The World Bank.

World Bank, 2000c, *World Development Report 1998/99: Knowledge for Development*, Washington, DC, The World Bank (http://www.worldbank.org/wdr/wdr98/contents.htm)

World Bank, *World Development Report 2000/2001: Attacking Poverty*, Washington, DC, World Bank (http://www.worldbank.org/poverty/wdrpoverty/

Wright, C. (ed.), 2000, *Issues in Education and Technology*, London, Commonwealth Secretariat.

Whyte, A. 1999, 'Understanding the Role of Community Telecentres in Development: A Proposed Approach to Evaluation' in Gomez R. and Hunt P (Eds).

Whyte, A., 2000, *Assessing Community Telecentres*, Ottawa, International Development Research Centre (IDRC).

Zongo, G., 2001, *Information and Communication Technologies for Development in Africa: Trends and Overview*, Turin, United Nations System Staff College (http://www.unssc.org/unscp/programmefocus/p2/knowledge_sharing/case_studies/IT_African_Development.PDF)

The Publishers

The **International Development Research Centre** is a public corporation created by the Parliament of Canada in 1970 to help developing countries use science and technology to find practical, long-term solutions to the social, economic, and environmental problems they face. Support is directed toward developing an indigenous research capacity to sustain policies and technologies developing countries need to build healthier, more equitable, and more prosperous societies.

IDRC Books publishes research results and scholarly studies on global and regional issues related to sustainable and equitable development. As a specialist in development literature, IDRC Books contributes to the body of knowledge on these issues to further the cause of global understanding and equity. IDRC publications are sold through its head office in Ottawa, Canada, as well as by IDRC's agents and distributors around the world. The full catalogue is available at http://www.idrc.ca/booktique/.

CODESRIA is the Council for the Development of Social Science Research in Africa head-quartered in Dakar, Senegal. It is an independent organisation whose principal objectives are facilitating research, promoting research-based publishing and creating multiple forums geared towards the exchange of views and information among African researchers. It challenges the fragmentation of research through the creation of thematic research networks that cut across linguistic and regional boundaries.

CODESRIA publishes a quarterly journal, *Africa Development*, the longest standing Africa-based social science journal; *Afrika Zamani*, a journal of history; the *African Sociological Review, African Journal of International Affairs (AJIA)* and *Identity, Culture and Politics: An Afro-Asian Dialogue*. Research results and other activities of the institution are disseminated through 'Working Papers', 'Monograph Series', 'New Path Series', 'State-of-the-Literature Series', 'CODESRIA Book Series', and the *CODESRIA Bulletin*.

Achevé d'imprimer
sur les presses de l'Imprimerie Saint-Paul
Angle rues El Hadj Mbaye Guèye (ex Sandiniéry) / Dr Thèze
DAKAR
Décembre 2003